A Lost Boy

One Man's Journey From Childhood Abuse
To Authentic Freedom

MIKE ROSSMAN

WESTBOW®
PRESS

A DIVISION OF THOMAS NELSON
& ZONDERVAN

WestBow Press books may be ordered through booksellers or by contacting:

WestBow Press
A Division of Thomas Nelson & Zondervan
1663 Liberty Drive
Bloomington, IN 47403
www.westbowpress.com
1 (866) 928-1240

ISBN: 978-1-4908-5006-1 (sc)
ISBN: 978-1-4908-5007-8 (hc)
ISBN: 978-1-4908-5008-5 (e)

Library of Congress Control Number: 2014915584

Printed in the United States of America.

WestBow Press rev. date: 09/04/2014

To my beautiful wife, Dusty, I thank God for giving you eyes to see and a heart to love unconditionally.

To my three amazing children, you are my greatest blessing, and I embrace the privilege of being your dad.

A special thanks also to my friend, Beaker!

CONTENTS

INTRODUCTION

WHEN PEOPLE ASKED WHAT my childhood was like, the answer always came easy.

"I don't remember."

I found it odd that they even asked. I am sure such questions are a normal part of the conversations most people have while getting to know one another. For me, the momentary reflection on my past and my inability to provide an honest answer would lead me to walk away with an unusually heavy burden. It was clear to me that I needed to avoid the topic altogether. Thus, I went to great lengths to remain secretive about my past, preferring to go unnoticed. My early years were a forbidden zone—all but forgotten. Yet the shadow of something dark, some secret I did not want to rediscover, remained.

On occasion, I would sense a clear yet subtle undertone in a conversation—an indefinable *something* provoking an unspoken and intangible connection. In those moments, I sensed a mutual understanding and the need to bypass small talk in an attempt to piece together the fractured parts of something shattered. Eventually, I realized my quiet demeanor communicated a presence assuring others that I already understood their painful secrets—even though I was nowhere near understanding my own.

When asked about my childhood, I always answered, "I don't remember," smiling with guarded anticipation and knowing such a simple response would not be sufficient. The problem was, if I attempted to answer truthfully, the emotional complexity intensified my confusion, and I quickly became stuck, unable to go back or move forward in my thoughts.

Over time, the questions about my childhood caused me to develop a defense in order to prevent an uprising of anxiety or a sense of obligation to go beyond my original response. I mastered the art of redirecting the focus away from me while at the same time giving my undivided attention to hearing another person's story. In fact, I felt a deep interest in other people's stories, and I remained engaged as they shared their hearts. Whether they told me fond memories of joy-filled experiences or those darker memories of violence and violation, I longed to hear the chronicles of their pasts. I didn't understand this urge at the time. Yet, I felt compelled to seek someone else's childhood story, to seek one I could adopt as my own. I resonated with the terrifying, but I yearned for the loving.

Over the years, the repetition of "I don't remember" caused me to believe my childhood had been lost and held no redemptive value. Because of this, after a while, I no longer felt concerned that someone would break the complicated code of untruth. So powerful are the mind's tactics for survival, I actually believed it was common for adults not to remember the first ten years of life. By completely discounting these precious years—the years God designed to enable little ones to learn to live in faith and wonder—I maintained an intentional disconnect. I needed to ensure a forgotten little boy would have no relevance to the man I became.

I reasoned to myself, *How can the fragile innocence and unashamed expectation of a child, who hopes to be a Jedi knight or a princess and to fully experience the bliss of barefoot summers, swimming pools, and puppy dogs, along with the most pure desire to be loved, become the unshakable foundation that can hold the weight of life?* To me it didn't make sense. I believed dreaming was dangerous, and I did not allow myself hope or joy. Such restraint was an exercise of strength and self-protection. Exercising my defenses daily allowed me to avoid being hurt or afraid.

For most of my life, I rigorously upheld and reinforced the vows I made in my heart as a boy. The declarations proved themselves an effective cushion against pain. Thus, I became a seasoned performer in a continuous battle between my untouchable secret, which I hid behind so many lies, and the force of a gentle and sovereign truth. This truth was, and still is, unwilling to leave behind a forgotten little boy, accepting no less than complete victory and authentic freedom for the man I have become. Though I said, "I don't remember my childhood," the truth would not let me forget, would not let go until I learned to love that little lost boy.

This is my story.

CHAPTER 1

─◄◦►─

Without Words

IN 2001, AT THE age of thirty-four, I began seeing a psychiatrist, desperately trying to overcome the pain of my divorce and the deep sadness I felt because my son, Cole, no longer lived with me. As a result, I discovered a preexisting and undefined terror within me that often triggered a loss of control in my life, rapidly accelerating into a freefall. I began to understand a little that the deep pain I felt was not the aftereffect of my ended marriage, but a buried wound suffered by a child I did not know. Because I was unwilling to venture into the abyss of my past, my psychotherapy sessions went dark and silent.

I made measurable breakthroughs related to my divorce; however, I could not break free from the overwhelming distress I continued to experience, which had initially surfaced after the magnificent birth of my son two years before. I possessed grave and unexplained concerns. *I don't want to bring a child into this world. I'm not going to be able to protect him.* Guilt over the precious gift of my son, Cole, consumed me, and the delicacy of his innocence only amplified my guilt. *I already failed to protect another little boy many years before,* I constantly reminded myself.

Months of therapy sessions went by. I would show up, close my eyes, and clench my jaw shut. Dr. Claremont occasionally interrupted the silence. "Where are you going?" he asked, aware I was escaping during these times when the room remained quiet, and my mind frantically searched for a safe place. I stayed motionless and quiet, struggling to find a way to communicate without speaking a word. *Don't give in,* I thought. I refused to release control by submitting to the doctor's expectation that I would talk.

The drawn-out periods of silence would eventually end when Dr. Claremont gently informed me my time was up. Hearing those specific words gave me the permission I needed to return from the place I had escaped to, and before leaving the psychiatrist's office, I would politely thank him, adding, "We are making excellent progress." I didn't want Dr. Claremont to give up on me. Every part of me believed the statement to be the farthest thing from the truth; nevertheless, Dr. Claremont agreed with my assessment. With his trained eye, he was witnessing the gradual erosion of my coping mechanisms, while he exercised patience in waiting to hear the secrets I privately committed to never share. Dr. Claremont knew I wanted to talk. He sensed my desperate need to tell. However, because I was unable to trust, he would have to wait. The test of his professional skill was going to be in direct relation to the depth of my betrayal. I was determined that I was not going to give up what I had tirelessly hidden for many years, even if it was going to kill me.

I initially began therapy in anticipation of a brief and painless exercise, a payment to confirm the cause of my depression—my ex-wife. *This will be quick, especially after I tell him what happened,* I thought. I needed his validation. However, my initial sessions led me in a different direction, and I found myself at a crossroads where both paths led to a loss of control—the control I needed to survive.

It was one thing to experience the immediate release of sharing built-up feelings with someone who skillfully guided me to the ledge of terrifying fear in an exercise of trust. Alone, my trust only took me so far. Once I was exposed and vulnerability struck, the loss of control felt worse than death. In the midst of this time, eerily familiar and unexplainable childlike habits began to surface. In isolation, I began to speak a form of gibberish I was surprisingly fluent in, and in private moments of anxiety, I would instinctively tell myself, "Don't worry; it's only pokido."

Am I insane? I wondered. Somehow, those simple words calmed the fierce intensity building inside me long enough for me to become who I needed to be—anyone other than me.

I wanted to be free, but I was convinced freedom would not be mine. This proved an effective barrier to healing and kept me spinning on the cycle between the revealed and the hidden. The truth is, had I been able to measure the cost of finding freedom before I started, I would have chosen to remain hopeless. My burning desire to be free would not have been worth the price. Fortunately, I didn't know how much it would hurt until it was too late to turn back.

Still, avoiding pain dictated every action and consumed every thought. I believed I was unlovable and alone, and all my decisions were based on survival and positioning myself in a controlled and safe dwelling place—a place existent only in my mind. To enter, I needed to be motionless and alone. In moments of terror, I envied those incarcerated for life and sentenced to solitary confinement. The world I lived in could easily fit into an eight-by-nine-foot room, and the three concrete walls and steel bars were exactly what I wanted—not to keep me in, but to keep others out. Prison would provide me the only freedom I could comprehend—freedom from what I believed others expected of me, such as living, succeeding, and worst of all, pretending I was okay.

When I went to psychotherapy, I set out to seek help in finding truth—an element so elusive throughout my life—and in the process, I unknowingly set a course to discover who I was. I disliked, even despised, where this path of discovery was leading. But it was simply too late to turn back.

My anxiety mounted daily. Increasingly, I felt trapped in a state of helplessness and affliction. It was all hauntingly familiar, and I suddenly began to resist entering Dr. Claremont's office alone. *How is this possible?* I wondered. I was a grown man, yet I was seeing from the perspective of a frightened child, a child who knew my fears better than I did. The good doctor was a gray-haired figure who waited for me to enter a room alone, and in the confines of a secretive place, I believed he would administer unspeakable pain.

Driving to my regularly scheduled appointment and believing I had no choice other than to go, I decided to stop for a drink. I was Clark Kent entering a telephone booth and walking out as Superman. At least, that's how it felt. I sheepishly entered the bar as a damaged and broken child in an oversized body, and after a few beers and a shot of whiskey, I walked out the doors feeling invincible—exactly how I thought a man should feel.

I was on to something. I had found help (or so I thought). I replaced the limited trust developed in Dr. Claremont and turned from his willingness to walk alongside me through the process of healing. In alcohol, I found an expedited and seemingly painless alleviation. Thus, when I entered Dr. Claremont's office, slightly buzzed, I went straight for the chair. I no longer felt any need to lie on the couch of vulnerability. "I am doing great today, Dr. Claremont, and I feel like all we have worked on has finally come together for me." The fear of him giving up on me was no longer a concern. I had convinced myself that he, and any others who falsely believed they could help me, would eventually fail. There was no hope for me.

Determined to remain in a state of deception and disconnect, I surrendered to the daily self-condemnation confirming my nothingness. I partnered with the one who welcomed my desire to die and entered into bondage with darkness, accepting the deadly terms. To me, the brief moments of relief that I relied on after the first drink were worth the price. I wasn't ready to end my life immediately, but I did willingly embrace hopelessness.

As an adult who had never developed healthy ways of dealing with life's adversities, I strived for significance to ensure my place of comfort and protection from everyday life. Therefore, I claimed hollow victories as often as I could. However, after I set the bar at death and my submission to the deceptively elusive sensation of alcohol masterfully disguised as peace, it became my one aim. I desperately chased this fleeting peace, seeing it always beyond my reach. Because I had given up hope, the fear of the consequences of my actions vanished, and my free will began a downfall that I had no intention of stopping.

"I no longer need therapy, Dr. Claremont, and I am going to try this on my own for a while." I made sure to tell him this immediately after he walked me into his office from the waiting room.

He agreed it was a good idea to stop. In his professional opinion, he had been successful in guiding me to the underlying source of pain. Although I felt it, I was not willing to look at it. He saw this too, and in concern, suggested I not remain there. I knew he saw something in me worth discovering for myself—something beyond the pain. But the problem was, I was convinced I would never be able to see it.

As far as I was concerned, this something never existed, and therefore it wasn't possible to find. Looking within was not possible for me. I could not even bear to glance into a mirror, which reflected back to me all my self-hatred. If I stared too long, I would literally punch myself in the face while clearly saying words I had heard a long time ago: "I am nothing and will always be nothing."

When I quit therapy, the hopeless place I found myself in was both surreal and memorable. The world finally paused long enough for me to realize my life would never be the same again. I could no longer pursue the image of who I wanted to be, and everything I had learned and created along the way became as worthless as me.

I believed I had fooled Dr. Claremont into thinking he was helping someone else, passing over me. It always needed to be someone other than me; I was beyond help. The person I saw in the mirror was hopeless and damaged beyond repair, and it was critical that the fatal wounds remained hidden. Over the course of my appointments, Dr. Claremont maintained his unwavering position that I deserved help. I deserved to be released and set free. He thought I had a chance at a real life and freedom.

In a sense, I did truly long to be free, but the terror I felt at the prospect of facing my pain with open eyes far exceeded my desire for freedom. Because I used the lies of my past to determine the value of my life, I was convinced that allowing light to shine brightly into my darkness would only reveal the weight and magnitude of what was lost. I never stood on solid ground. Even if I did find the strength to stand and the courage to open my eyes, I knew the burden would be too heavy. If I finally accepted the truth about the events of my past, I would not be able to lift it, and I certainly would not be able to carry it alone. Burrowing deeper into despair was familiar and felt safe. I had never known anything else.

I was like an inmate who served a long sentence, institutionalized within the dark and unforgiving walls of prison. Eventually, the payment of suffering is satisfactory to repay the debt to society, and the prisoner enters a world that is unwilling to wait for him, a world unlike the one he once knew. It is a terrifying discovery. The harsh reality leads some to commit another crime in order to return to the safety of a dangerous place.

I, too, wanted to return to the safety of a private and personal affliction, where I had mastered survival.

CHAPTER 2

—◄○►—

Take a Drink

THROUGH PSYCHOTHERAPY, A CHILDHOOD wound was touched, and my adult mind raced to find a way to cope. I turned to the only means I believed was available—alcohol! Exercising my free will in a sober state was nearly impossible. Though I had attempted it countless times before, I determined once again, with increased determination, to start over. It was my only option. Starting over was always the answer. It bypassed the necessary pain involved in healing. Instead of going deeper and sorting through the darkness of my childhood, I thought I could take a shortcut. If I intentionally disconnected from the pain, I could make a sprint to an end, motivated by fear, until I could no longer breathe. Thus, I stood at the doorway of my prison cell, still shackled with fear. In a dark and narrow place, I had to choose between the painful and liberating path to freedom and the dead end road of self-reliance fueled by alcohol. I chose alcohol. I believed I had found the answer.

Until the day I ended therapy and no longer sought help but instead chose alcohol, I had never taken the time to measure how much energy, how many resources, and how much life I wasted looking for identity and acceptance. Everything I did revolved around this need: forget the past, move on, become popular at school, become an athlete, go to college, get in better shape, become successful in business, read a self-help book, get married, accumulate stuff, and make friends to compare the stuff. For a short time these things seemed to work, yet the emptiness remained and intensified. The promise of genuine happiness, peace, and security never materialized. Instead, I began to realize the true cost—the debts I had accumulated in an elusive pursuit.

Those close to me, relatively speaking, began communicating their concern over how much time and money I spent on therapy, particularly as they observed my outward health and appearance deteriorate. I listened, sensing their concern revealed their underlying need for me to resume my futile pursuit of what the world promises. They needed to confirm that they too were on the right track. How could I blame them for this when I looked to them for the same assurance? Based on our carefully constructed facades, we were all doing well and racing toward the next benchmark in life, confident it would provide the missing peace in our lives.

As I left psychotherapy, I declared another do-over for my life. I reentered the race. The starting line was a well-deserved vacation in the Bahamas at an all-inclusive resort offering an endless indulgence in food, alcohol, and escape. When I arrived, I sat in my hotel room alone and afraid. I considered cancelling and returning home. This was my familiar dilemma: No matter where I was, there I was. The change of venue could not change the battle raging within me.

Finally, I worked up the courage to leave the room. I headed to the pool, stopping by one of the many bars to order a beer. Arriving at my lounge chair, I felt like everyone was watching me, like my life and problems were somehow transparent—until I took a drink. I could not get the bottle to my lips fast enough. I felt like Pigpen from the Peanuts, who walks covered by a visible cloud of filth.

However, the cold beer ignited a transformation in me. I had an endless supply of beer and an environment promoting drunkenness morning, day, and night. Quickly, I felt I belonged. After four beers, I could easily start a conversation and begin establishing who I was not. I began making vacation friends, as I was able to do many times in the past. With the aid of alcohol, I was able to fit in. Alcohol, for me, was a countermeasure to paralysis, and once I had enough, I finally felt free to experience the things that I always avoided. My life had no middle ground. I was either sober and terrified or fearless and intoxicated. I was not afraid of dying but only of suffering.

One afternoon, I set out on a run to explore the Bahamas existing behind the manicured beach resorts. It is common knowledge that tourists are safe within a perimeter around the resorts. However, it typically is not a good idea to go beyond the boundaries. I didn't care. I was fully committed to seeking out the hidden realities of people's lives. Before I was able to break a sweat, I came across a few locals who waved me down, "Hey, man. Come on over here and join us for a shot of whiskey." I accepted and felt more at ease than I did approaching someone poolside at the resort. It was not a safe situation, but I felt comfort in knowing my fear was justified. My greatest fear was of not being able to see the danger.

The cheap booze helped me ease into small talk with the three men and one woman. Within the time it took me to throw back four shots of whiskey, I could see the woman was getting uncomfortable for my sake. Her concern increased as the men kept offering me shots, and I kept accepting. Increasingly, the men began to discuss things between themselves and laugh—intentionally leaving me out of the conversation.

"Just leave him alone," she told them.

I remained focused on the woman. Even though I was drunk, I sensed things would turn either weird or violent if I stayed. I casually thanked them for the whiskey and stumbled off to resume my run.

My brush with danger left me exhilarated. An encounter with clear and immediate danger felt much safer than the hidden dangers in institutions, reputations, rules, and moral authority. Instead of feeling concerned for what could have happened, I felt empowered and carefree. I loved not being afraid, and I was willing to risk everything to experience fear's absence.

I drank nonstop until I took the shuttle back to the airport to return home. While in the Bahamas, I experienced uninterrupted transformation for days. For the first time in my life, I had gone days without needing to fend off a constant offensive, which was present throughout my life. Without interruption, I could be someone else as long as I kept drinking. This experience settled it. I believed alcohol cleansed the filth covering me on the outside and neutralized the festering rot on the inside. My strategy was simple enough. I would bring my Bahamas experience home.

In real life, I was one of two partners in a real estate development firm. My responsibility was to create projects, work with the architect/engineers, raise private capital, secure bank financing, and work closely with government officials, city planners, and building departments. I was thorough and effective, driven by a deep passion to create buildings that I had dreamed about as a child.

It all began when, as a five-year-old boy, I experienced hope while watching Sesame Street. The source of my hope wasn't Big Bird, Grover, or any of the other characters; it was the street itself. I wanted to live on such a street. Sesame Street was a safe place where family and friends worked in the marketplace below and lived in the apartments above. Kids were free to play and explore within a community of moms, dads, grandparents, friends, and creatures who loved, protected, and cared for children. Kids were safe there, so I promised myself I would live there one day.

The city I lived in did not have such a place. As an adult, I set out to build it myself. I lived my dream and vision through developing mid-rise buildings, complete with ground floor retail and multi-levels of housing above.

First Phase of Sesame St. Built in 2000

The communities would be secure, and because of their reputation for safety, they would be vibrant and full of life. When completed, the buildings would promote family in the truest sense and be free from the crime and domestic issues destroying many others.

Before going into business meetings, I often felt inadequate, and I could not understand why the people I met with on a regular basis showed me respect and shared my excitement for my vision. I made sure not to disclose my dream of building Sesame Street, knowing it would undermine the credibility I had somehow gained. As meetings progressed, my nervousness would dissipate, and I focused my attention on what I was going to accomplish. It took perseverance to overcome my fears, but my belief was strong, so I made sure I found a way to fulfill my dream.

After returning from the Bahamas, I was no longer willing to work through the initial stages of self-doubt I would experience while attending meetings and making important decisions. I began stopping at a bar first to have a few drinks. Hiding my new partnership with alcohol was easier than hiding the guilt, shame, and unworthiness I felt when I was sober. Because I had spent my life hiding, I was well equipped to conceal the effects of alcohol. As I returned to "normal" life, my desperate need to avoid fear quickly returned. I began waking up terrified each morning, which created a building anxiety in me, rooted in the anticipation of daily morning terror. The demons from my past were relentless and opportunistic. They always seemed to know when to attack. As soon as I awoke, before I could assemble my defenses, the terror would hit with deadly precision. This daily bombardment left me at the mercy of a familiar adversary. In time, I began taking an immediate shot of morning whiskey.

Over thirty years of pretending I was normal, I had developed a determination to function at a calculated level in every aspect of my life, even in the midst of my progressing addiction. I tried to remain focused on work and spending time with my son, Cole, yet my ability to function as a dad was the first and most important area to show signs of cracking. Cole was becoming too much for me to handle. My inability had nothing to do with Cole's behavior. He was a sweet child whom I loved, and I wanted nothing more than to freely experience the joy and privilege of being his dad. Instead, I found myself paralyzed.

Cole was beautiful in every way, though when I looked into his eyes, I became overwhelmed with sadness. His tiny figure was an embodiment of childhood innocence and truth, and I saw in him my own conflict. My contention, stirred by lies, brought forward a past I had vowed never to think of again. Thus, Cole's presence challenged my self-hate by touching the core of my soul's created essence. He reminded me of what my childhood should have been but never was.

Over a span of three decades, I had built walls to contain how I felt about myself, except those walls began to crumble in the presence of my son. He reminded me of all I had lost, and I found it impossible to separate yet secure the love I had for him. It was a love a father has for his child, and it was not to be contained. Although love interceded, the unhealed wounds of my soul rejected it as a defense to the feelings I was unable to process. For this reason alone, I found it hard to be around Cole. In the face of my inability to be the father I wanted to be, I turned again to my liquid comfort.

CHAPTER 3

◄(O)►

Two Hurts Together

BECAUSE OF MY FEAR of intimacy, I held little value for relationships. I didn't value myself, and I could not value others. As a result, I recklessly decided to begin dating. I figured whoever entered my life would need to leave it within six months. I always made sure it happened. My singles dating profile would have read something like:

> *Single Alcoholic Male with Deep Issues He's Not Fully Aware of: Looking for single female wanting a minimum ten years of unbridled chaos, heartbreak, and dysfunction before things get better. No guarantees!*

Equipped with my false freedom, I met a beautiful woman named Dusty. I had one thing going for me; I was beyond believing another person could fill the emptiness in my life. Alcohol was filling the void.

When we first met, I felt an instant attraction to Dusty. Although she was pretty and did enjoy many of the activities I liked, there was something deeper drawing me to her. An affinity subconsciously draws two damaged souls together. Our connection had two potential outcomes. Either we would elevate our already toxic and dysfunctional lives to new levels of misery or, through a miracle, we would set an unfamiliar course by forming a partnership allowing enough grace for restoration and wholeness in both of us. I didn't know it at the time, but when I met Dusty, I was embarking on the journey toward a miracle.

I would like to say we experienced the miracle in our relationship from the beginning, but my claim would be a lie. Our life together began without any resistance to the shadow of generational dysfunctions we both lived under. We inherited the need and an obligation to unleash unresolved pain on to each other.

Dusty worked at my sister Lori's salon as a hairstylist, and her personality was the opposite of mine. Dusty was vibrant and loved to talk. In fact, because of her volume, she was relegated to a private soundproof room in the salon. Because she was a masterfully skilled hairstylist, her clients felt exquisitely transformed after sitting in her chair. I am convinced it had more to do with their time spent with Dusty than the dazzling makeover.

In those days, I still had hair, and I went to Dusty for a regular haircut. Dusty would sit me down in her chair, and while she cut and styled my hair, we would talk. Mostly she talked while I listened in awe. I had never met anyone who had so much to say. The best part though was when she brushed up against me, and a warm, excited feeling rushed through me. I did not feel comfortable with physical touch, yet with Dusty, it was different. Of course, I did not tell her as much.

We began spending our free time together, most of it during happy hour. Dusty was unaware of the extent of my drinking problem; however, it wasn't long before I stopped trying to hide it from her. To my surprise, Dusty often kept up with my pace. Apparently, for both of us there was never enough alcohol to take the pain away.

Our relationship evolved into a sexual one quickly, even though intimacy and physical relationships were extremely difficult for me. I doubt I had ever experienced true intimacy. I rarely even experienced sex without being under the influence of alcohol. I liked Dusty and felt comfortable around her. Still, my deep issues affected our relationship. Because our painful life experiences went unattended, we remained broken. We could hardly mature into a committed and loving couple, let alone prepare for what happened next.

One day I received a phone call from Dusty. She was crying. After struggling to get the words out, she said, "I'm pregnant."

We had been dating nine months. I believed the relationship was predetermined to fail, so I responded with intentional ambiguity. "Everything will be okay," I reassured her.

To me, the words I spoke were to communicate we would not be having the child. To Dusty, it meant the opposite. In the midst of my increased anxiety and sadness about falling short as a dad to Cole, I knew I needed to make my position clear. I refused to be a part of bringing another child into this messed-up world. I wholeheartedly believed it was too dangerous, and I knew I lacked the capacity to provide the protection a child would need.

Today, I cannot fathom the decisive disregard I felt toward the life of our child, even while I was incredibly lost and unsure in everything else. *Where did I get this false authority to impose a sentence of death? What future hope and impact might this child have in other people's lives? How would this affect Dusty?* I never even considered these questions. I placed no value on life. I made a judgment out of the evil in my heart that made more sense out of death than life.

Cold-faced and with a complete lack of emotion, I briefly and firmly let Dusty know, "I do not want you to have our baby." I rationalized my decision further by adding, "My life is out of control, and I cannot be responsible for another child." She remained quiet while fighting back tears and accepted my non-negotiable position. My choice determined the fate of our child. A silent cloud hung over us through the planning of the abortion, and an even darker silence came on the day of the execution, introducing a season of destruction. I did not realize the decimating impact of what I had done for some time. The death of our daughter, whom Dusty wanted to name Ava, became another buried secret in my life.

CHAPTER 4

—◄○►—

There and Back Again

AFTER THE ABORTION, I became even more dependent on alcohol. My emotions began to churn with a conviction I could not withstand, and I tried all I could to drown them out. I felt completely out of control, eventually calling Dr. Claremont again. During an episode of uncontrollable crying, I told him, "It hurt so bad."

Not knowing what "it" was, Dr. Claremont asked, "Have you been drinking?"

I said, "Yes."

He suggested I come in for an appointment the following day. "Do your best not to drink beforehand," he said, and I agreed.

I endured a few silent and sober sessions with Dr. Claremont, although my attempts were feeble, and it wasn't long before I showed up drunk.

"Have you been drinking?" he asked immediately after stepping into the privacy of his office.

"Yes," I replied, without any attempt to hide it.

"Mike, our time together will not be effective as long as you continue to self-medicate," he firmly stated, with an undertone of frustration. Prior to turning to alcohol, I had been committed to the painful work, yet now I was in the grip of addiction, and by this time it was clear I would not be able to stop on my own. Dr.

Claremont suggested I seek help through a treatment center, and I agreed to look into it.

I made an appointment with a local facility, and Dusty lovingly escorted me to the location of the thirty-day program. My motivation for checking in was misdirected toward a focus on controlling my drinking and not on discovering hope in sobriety. I needed what alcohol could do for me, and I was unwilling to let it go entirely. If I lost all the coping skills I had developed over the years, I believed I would also lose control. I didn't think it was possible to function without it. All I wanted was to find a way to control when, where, and how much I drank, therefore regaining the ability to silence the voices in my head long enough for me to be a good dad to my son Cole. If I was unable to get my drinking under control, Cole's mom would have a justifiable and convincing reason not to trust me with our son. This was the last thing I wanted.

The treatment center was part of a medical group where my ex-wife worked as an ER nurse. By this time, we were arguing over issues related to visitation with Cole. *What if she finds out I am an alcoholic and have been admitted for treatment?* I wondered. My uneasiness relating to Cole had continued to increase as he became older, and through a series of cancellations—both on my ex-wife's part and more increasingly on my own—my ability to keep it together for Cole was unraveling.

I was surprised at how quickly I adjusted to the routine of inpatient care over the first few days of the program. The effects of feeling safe outweighed the suffering from withdrawal symptoms. I felt comfortable with the other patients, given we all had a commonality in pain and a drug of choice to mask the underlying issues. I listened to testimonies of hitting rock bottom, how they had arrived, and the need for a higher power in their lives. I sat and listened intently but rejected what I heard about "the only way" to be sober.

It wasn't resentment or pride (although those certainly existed) preventing me from seeking freedom from addiction; it was an unwillingness to take a thorough and fearless inventory of my life. I firmly believed that the consequences of doing so would be far worse than the consequences of my drunken state. *My situation is different from the others,* I reminded myself. The prospect of sharing with another person the secrets I had vowed never to tell was much worse than the loss of relationships, financial security, or reputation. My greatest fear was my own internal suffering.

On the fourth day, I received confirmation it was already time for me to leave. When I heard a knock on the door to my room, I answered it to find a priest dressed in his vestment.

"Would you like to spend a few minutes talking?" the older religious man asked.

Slightly dazed by his presence, I quickly replied, "No!"—not allowing him an opportunity to talk beyond his question. Without a word, he turned and moved on to the next door. In an uncharacteristically decisive move, I quickly gathered my belongings and checked out. I didn't fully understand why, and I didn't care.

After exiting the recovery program, I quickly picked up where I had left off in my addiction. I continued going to therapy appointments, though less frequently, and when I did go, I sat on the chair rather than lying on the couch. I was rigidly defensive and intentionally shallow, limiting what I said to current issues and updates on my drinking. Determinedly, I attempted to build my emotional foundation upon the quicksand of my life. Despair became my comfort. It was far better than uncovering my childhood and sifting through painful truths and lies.

After one of my regularly-scheduled appointments with Dr. Claremont, for which I managed to stay sober, I headed directly to the bar. Our afternoon's discussion had been like all the others of late. I had stirred distracting surface issues to trouble and confuse me in a calculated way. My sole intention was to remain disconnected from my past—disconnected from truth. In a backwards way, the money and time I wasted on therapy at this stage, due to my own choices, served one purpose. It amplified my symptoms enough to justify my self-prescribed medication, which seemed to be more effective.

When I arrived at the bar, I ordered a beer and a shot of whiskey, quickly drank both, and ordered another beer. I felt the alcohol warm my veins and calm my nerves, and I asked the bartender for the newspaper, as I typically did. Reading about the most recent murderers, rapists, and white collar criminals who faced justice seemed to help me feel better about myself.

I unfolded the paper to reveal the front page. A bold headline sprawled across the top: NEW ROUND OF MOLESTATION FILINGS ACCUSES FIVE PRIESTS FROM OREGON. Suddenly, everything changed. Breathless, I read a few more paragraphs and drank a lot more whiskey. Despite the alcohol, the truths I had buried deeply in my subconscious began to resurface at a rapid pace. Vivid and terrifying details played before me.

Suddenly, I remembered.

CHAPTER 5

—◄○►—

Learning to Forget

I LOVE MY MOM and dad and always have. How I love them has changed over the years.

My mom was nineteen and my dad was twenty when my sister, Lori, was born. I came along eighteen months later. Raising us was a tremendous responsibility for two young parents, particularly since they both carried their individual burdens from growing up in difficult home environments. Each had little time to find truth in their own lives before marriage and the birth of children. The baseline from which they set out to start our family was a deep level of pain. The specifics and magnitude of their childhood struggles, for the most part, went unspoken. My parents possessed a fierce reluctance about discussing difficult and painful situations, and it was clear to my sister and me that we needed to avoid such subjects.

I saw how my mom and dad presented themselves outwardly to others, and I knew it was an intentional deflection to protect what they battled internally—even though I was unclear what the conflict was about. Often, I felt frustrated by their avoidance of difficult questions and their refusal to seek answers for why life was hard. I needed them to see their own pain so they could see mine.

Because of their refusal to face pain, my parents blamed money for most of the problems in our home, and I learned there wasn't enough to overcome circumstances, anxiety, and anger. Although my parents remained married and lived in the same house, their past wounds, overshadowed by a spirit of poverty, kept them divided. Their lives revolved around the belief that they were missing out on what the world told them they needed. Thus, they were perpetually distracted with acquiring more stuff, which caused them to leave their priceless treasures unattended.

I don't know much about my mom's upbringing beyond the fact her parents were alcoholics. Her mother, diagnosed as terminally ill while my mom was still a child, faced a grim future, and she drank to cope with the hopelessness in her life. My mom's father, a veteran of World War II, also drank to keep away the tormenting memories of the war. My mom summarized her childhood simply by telling me she had felt nonexistent, and her silent cries went unheard.

My dad's upbringing was not any better. Over the years, he has shared a few of his experiences with me, and he still harbors anger and hatred toward his dad, even though he passed away many years ago. Those feelings were in contrast to the love and affection he felt toward his mom, who had provided for the family by working long hours in her beauty salon. My dad referred to his dad as an asshole, describing the verbal and physical abuse he had suffered. Unemployed most of his life, my grandfather had stayed home and drank until he had become violent, taking his aggression out on his defenseless son, often beating him with his belt. My dad's only fond memory of his father is the day he fought back as a teenager and told his dad if he ever touched him again he would kill him. After the confrontation, his dad diverted his violence and avoided striking out verbally or physically against my dad. It was a resentful remedy used to treat the symptoms of a furious disease, except it was (as it always is) ineffective in stopping the progression of terminal hate. It ensured the unresolved anger remained and carried forward in one form or another to the next generation.

As a child, I recall looking at my parents, and at no time did I consider they were anything other than my mom and dad. From the beginning, I believed the sole purpose and devotion of my parents, to whom I naturally looked to for all childhood desires and needs, was to love and protect my sister and me. I believed the two of them were fully equipped to know us, guide us, and love us unconditionally. Each child is born with a beautiful birthright and expectation. The fact that children know it and expect it can only mean each one of us, at some point, knew how valuable we were. Like all other children, I came into this world expecting good things in life. My life began with a foundational truth and an understanding of what is good and pleasing. But one day my life changed. Overtaken by an event, my innocence shifted to timidity undergirded by terror.

After the devastating event, I needed my mom and dad to notice something was terribly wrong with me, but unfortunately, my outward struggles looked normal through their broken lenses. Fear, unworthiness, and pain occupied our home and were given authority to raise my sister and me. It was all my mom and dad had ever known; anything else would have stood out. Instead, they regularly told my sister and me to forget about the past and move on. I took their advice and became an expert at forgetting (though I was as unsuccessful as my parents at actually moving on). In fact, I was so good at forgetting that after a while, I couldn't remember.

Then, one day in a bar, I opened a newspaper, and all I had forgotten washed over me in one terrible flood.

CHAPTER 6

◄○►

What the Boy Forgot

THIS IS WHAT I remembered.

One day, when I was four years old, my sister, Lori, and I found ourselves entrusted in the care of our grandfather, my dad's dad. He and my grandma lived close to us, and with my grandma away at work, we were alone with him. As soon as we arrived, my grandfather told Lori to go upstairs and not come down until he called for her. He then grabbed me by the arm and marched me in silent authority to the basement, where he sexually abused me.

When my mom and dad said good-bye to me that day, they had no idea of the enormity of all they were letting go of as the door closed behind them.

I had no ability to process what was happening. My senses grabbed on to little details in an effort to cope with the terror. All these years later, I can still hear the creaking of the old exposed wooden steps leading to the stained concrete floor. I can smell the thick and musty air and the distinctive smell of an alcoholic. I can feel the cold white freezer he laid me face down on and the overpowering presence of evil. For years, every old house, stairway, basement, and gray-haired old man ignited terror in my heart. Though I had forgotten why these things were terrifying, the broken places in my subconscious mind would trigger paralysis and an immediate shut down of my thought process.

When he was done, he told me to put my clothes back on and then struck me with a belt, reinforcing his demand that I keep my mouth shut. It is difficult to say for sure, but I believe my grandfather's unsatisfied and misdirected hate toward my dad resulted in his calculated assault on me. Even more uncertain was who first unleashed fury from an unresolved wound onto my grandfather. I cannot help wondering how far back the first secret of abuse goes in our family. Has anyone ever asked? Why didn't anyone ever scream and break the secret curse of silence?

My sister and I, separated from the watchful eyes of our parents, were alone with him at least three times, and each time the terrifying acts occurred. Then, although I did not tell my parents what had happened, for some unexplained reason, my grandfather's unsupervised access to my sister and me ended. However, it was too late for me. The innocent and carefree little boy I had been was gone forever. On some level, I believe my mom knew something had changed in me. I went silent and was terrified, though to most, I simply seemed to be a shy little boy.

Occasionally, we would visit my grandparents for family gatherings. As I walked in the door, my grandfather would look straight at me from his recliner with a glare to remind me to keep my mouth shut. It worked. I never said a word. Still, I hated my grandfather's house, and I hated having to go there. When I was five, I started to avoid going into their home, choosing to sit alone on a bench at a city park located across the street.

One day, while I sat waiting for my parents' call to leave, I noticed something flopping around in a fir tree. Frightened of what it could be, I approached with caution, poised to run at the first sign of danger. As I got closer, I could see someone had tied fishing line around the feet of a crow; the other end was tied to a branch, leaving the bird hanging upside down in a hopeless struggle for its life. Paralyzed with indecision, I wondered, *Should I save his life, or walk away and pretend I didn't see it?* It seemed easier to ignore it and move on. However, the crow saw me standing there, and as I witnessed the injuries he continued to inflict on himself, I knew I had to do something. I did the one thing I was unable to do for myself. I ran to get my dad's help. My dad was always willing to help injured and defenseless animals, and he didn't let me down. After I explained to him what I had seen, he led me without a word back across the street.

Firmly holding the bird in one hand, my dad cut the line with a pocketknife. With a concentrated furor, he scanned the park, wanting to take down the one responsible for such cruelty. He found no one, and the ruthless and cowardly act went unpunished. At moments like this, my dad never appeared afraid and always seemed to know what to do. I like to think we made a good team rescuing the crow, because after my dad released it from the tree, his focus was on hanging a man for the injustice, and mine was on whether the bird would live or die.

The crow had damaged both wings in his struggle for freedom, and left alone and unprotected, he was going to die. I was thrilled to accept the full responsibility of caring for the bird, whom I named Blackie. Having Blackie gave me something to look forward to in the morning, something to focus on before the sadness and fear took over. I woke up early each day to check on Blackie and followed my dad's instructions on how to keep him alive. The first thing I needed to do was to get the crow to eat and drink water, otherwise he would not survive. But no matter what I held in front of his beak, Blackie would not eat. I understood. I didn't like to eat either. Thoughts about the coming day's affliction filled my stomach with pain, making it difficult to swallow.

When I went to bed each night, Blackie was the last thing on my mind before I fell asleep. I imagined he was terrified all alone in our garage. I didn't want him to be afraid, and more than anything, I wanted him to trust me. It was important to me that Blackie knew I would not hurt him. I wanted Blackie to be free. When I picked him up, which he allowed me to do without any pecking or struggle, and put him on the concrete floor of our garage, where he could become familiar with his surroundings, he stood motionless at my feet. Eventually, I carried him outside. There Blackie followed me around the yard, seeming to sense my presence provided protection. For the first time, I experienced what it was like to be big.

I did my best to reassure Blackie he was going to get better, and when he did, I would set him free. At a young age, I possessed a deep understanding of what it was like to lose freedom, even though I didn't really know what freedom was.

I had Blackie for about two weeks. I enjoyed taking care of him, yet most of all, I enjoyed being his protector. Each morning, I jumped out of bed to check on my bird, seeking to reassure him that I hadn't forgotten him. I knew I would miss Blackie, but more than wanting to keep him, I wanted to prove that I meant what I said. I knew birds were born to fly and not to live in a box. I hoped for the restoration of Blackie's gift of flight and imagined how I would be the one to release it. I daydreamed about him returning often from his adventures, and I even wondered if someday I could teach him to talk. If parrots could talk, why couldn't Blackie? Deep down, I really wanted to hear him tell me I was the one who saved his life.

But Blackie was dead.

CHAPTER 7

—◄○►—

And So It Goes

WHILE I WAS STILL in my fifth year of life, our family moved about thirty miles from our old neighborhood, and the infrequent visits to my grandma and grandpa's became even more infrequent. This move was a sort of new beginning for all of us. We moved on in hopes of a better life, wanting to leave the past behind.

My dad worked long hours in a physically demanding trade as a framing contractor. However, I was too young to understand how hard he labored to provide for our family. To me, he always seemed to be far away, almost nonexistent. The quintessential man's man of the 1970s, my dad would do what was normal for men in construction at the time—go to the local tavern at the end of the day to unwind and shed the residual foul language and hardened shell required on the job site. I do not recall my dad ever coming home drunk. At no time did he come home and be belligerent or abusive toward my sister and me. I think he enjoyed the camaraderie and bond that develops through a group of men working together to build something tangible.

Life was different for my mom, who was the complete opposite of my dad. She preferred the familiarity and comfort of home and absolutely hated the outdoors—especially hunting and fishing. At times, my mom struggled desperately with depression and found it difficult to make friends, spending the majority of her days in isolation. I'm not entirely sure why my mom didn't have her driver's license, but her inability to drive contributed to her aloneness. It also caused her to rely on others for transportation, not only for herself but for my sister and me.

Even at a young age, I noticed the differences between my mom and dad, but I never wondered why they were married. There was no reason to wonder. They were simply my mom and dad. From my perspective, they made complete sense, and I somehow knew the reason it was important for them to remain together. However, for them, the hopeful season of courtship, attraction, and commitment to one another had faded and been forgotten.

Shortly after we moved into our new home, my mom signed me up for kindergarten at the neighborhood church, St. Anne's, which was located a few miles from our house. She enrolled Lori in first grade at the public school, within walking distance, and Lori made the short journey with other children from the neighborhood. She also attended St. Anne's after school for Confraternity of Christian Doctrine (CCD) classes. Because St. Anne's was too far for us to walk to, various neighbors provided transportation.

Our next door neighbor had recommended the St. Anne's kindergarten to my mom and offered to provide transportation for me. He had the same name as our black lab—Yogi—though I definitely liked our dog better. My quick, childlike discernment was later confirmed when I found out our neighbor was a mean alcoholic who took pleasure in beating his five sons on a regular basis. I stood in our front yard and witnessed some of it. Mostly though, I would hear the violence coming from inside their home—doors slamming, screaming, foul language, and the sounds of a beating. On occasion, one of the younger boys, maybe a few years older than me, would run out the front door and abruptly stop at the curb, directly in front of his house. As he breathed rapidly, his watery eyes would connect with mine. I could tell he knew there was nowhere to run.

With the advent of kindergarten, my life settled into a routine of trying to remain unseen. Because of my grandfather's abuse, I was terrified everywhere. Being in an unfamiliar church environment only amplified my fears. Whenever people directed their attention my way, I immediately shut down. Riding to school in the neighbor's car triggered the onset of paralysis, and I do not recall ever saying a word. Being loaded into a vehicle and driven to a different location always created a danger in my mind—an opportunity for something bad to happen.

In kindergarten, I liked crafts and story time. Creativity calmed me, and I felt peace while listening to Ms. Littleton read. Best of all, during those two activities, my participation with others was not expected; instead, I was required to be quiet. Rules weren't necessary to keep me silent, but when all the kids had to be quiet, it was easier for me to blend in. When the other children laughed and played, I became extremely uncomfortable. I knew it caused me to stand out, and Ms. Littleton might notice I wasn't joining in. As a result, she often asked if something was wrong, which always caused me to cry, indicating something was, in fact, terribly wrong. It didn't matter. I knew to keep my mouth shut.

Enormous fir trees stood on the St. Anne's playground, and I developed a sense of safety in their presence. I would often stand at the base of one of the massive trunks, beneath the covering of gently swaying branches, and breathe in the pleasant smell of fir needles. Sometimes, I would lay down, becoming comfortably lost in their presence while blocking out the sounds of laughter coming from the other kids. I had no interest in playing with my classmates and always felt nervous they would invite me to join in. I couldn't understand why they were not scared, why they felt wholly free to run, jump, and scream with unashamed abandon.

Eventually the car rides with my neighbor and my time in kindergarten became familiar, even though I remained nervous and still refused to say a word. One time, while sitting in the back seat of our neighbor's car, scared, quiet, and feeling as if I was committing the crime of the century, I wiped a freshly picked booger under the seat. At once, I felt a small sense of control in a world in which I had none. I willed my secret strike against the man who owned the car and beat on his boys. It was my own secret, but it came with a price. *What if the man finds my booger?* For months I obsessed about the discovery of the booger, and I played out the countless forms of impending punishment in my mind. It didn't cross my mind that, with five boys in their family, it would have been difficult for them to stick this one on me.

When I was not in school, I would venture into our neighborhood to play by myself. It didn't take long for the neighborhood bullies to spot my weak and fragile demeanor. I eventually learned that feeling like a target tends to make you one. My first encounter with the neighborhood bully, Darrel, involved his BB gun. Darrel lived on a dead end street, and passing his house once meant there was no escaping passing it again. He shot me as I raced by in both directions. I returned home crying, displaying the minor welts from the BBs, and my dad immediately marched down to Darrel's house. I didn't dare watch, but when my dad returned, I heard him tell my mom he had ripped the gun out of the kid's hands and broken it in two over his knee.

My dad harbored a fierce temper, but except for appropriate discipline, my sister and I were never recipients of my dad's wrath. However, I did witness it on occasion. One time, our family was together in the car with my dad driving when another car cut directly in front of him. Immediately I felt nervous, knowing my dad was unable to let such things go. This time was no different. My dad honked the horn, which by my dad's standards was not an excessive retaliation—enough to let the guy know he was a little too close.

At the next stop light, while the car my dad honked at was next to us, the driver flipped my dad off. The finger, witnessed by all, appeared in midair for what seemed like an hour. I hoped the light would quickly change to green, but it was too late. My dad was already out of our car. The light was still red, and the man in the other car was frantically trying to manually roll up his window (remember, it was the 1970s) before my dad arrived. He did get his window up in time, but it didn't matter. My dad's giant fist went right through the thick glass, and the momentum carried his hand forward directly to the man's collar and throat. I imagine it was somewhat like the time when my dad told his father he would kill him.

Quickly releasing the driver of the other car from his grip, my dad calmly walked back to our car. We drove off in silence. Back then, men confronted each other without deadly intent. There was no exchanging of insurance information, no gunfire, and no pending lawsuit for the pain and damage caused by a negligent fist. Only two grown men acting out their secret hurt at a random intersection.

My dad could be extremely intimidating, yet even after his imposing figure bore down on the ten-year-old boy, breaking the BB gun in two, Darrel continued to come after me. On one particular spring day, I was out enjoying a peaceful ride on my bike when I noticed Darrel watching me. He was not doing anything, just watching. The lack of action scared me. After I built up the courage and enough speed to ride past him, it became painfully clear why Darrel had waited so patiently. He had strung fishing line across the street, attaching it to two trees. His calculations were spot on. As I cycled by, the line cut in across my neck until my momentum caused the invisible line to snap. I returned home crying with a welt and a cut wrapped halfway around my neck. My dad wasn't home from work yet, although when he arrived, I heard my mom talking to him. Then I heard the door slam. I don't know what happened; what I do know is Darrel's crosshairs found a new target.

Then there was Buddy. I could not understand how a kid could be so tough and mean. Initially, he contained his harassment to teasing and verbal threats. That changed one day when, enraged at his taunts, I ran toward him swinging. I cannot recall what set me off; it must have been something special. I didn't know I had it in me. At first he let me hit him, probably for the shear amusement of how much it didn't hurt, and once he'd had enough, he grabbed my arm and flung me across the yard, dislocating my shoulder. I went home crying—*again!*

Prior to Buddy's stepped-up aggression, my dad made friends with Buddy's dad, and although my dad chose not to do anything to his friend's boy, he apparently said something to his friend. I was standing in my front yard shortly after the incident, my arm in a sling, and I witnessed Buddy taking a beating from his dad with a large wooden spoon. It was one of those heavy, oversized spoons used for serving salad, which in the early 1970s meant that the spoon was huge and certainly made out of real wood, with possible traces of lead. As Buddy screamed and pleaded for his dad to stop, something came over me. I felt scared for Buddy. I cried for him, noticing he did not cry for himself. I realized this was a familiar routine for Buddy, and I knew the wrong person had received the punishment.

Throughout my experiences at school and with the neighborhood bullies, I always sought a safe place but never found one. I was tired of both the perceived and real threats I was sure followed me, and I felt incapable of discerning between the two. The only semblance of safety I found was on Sesame Street. Watching it, I felt hope that such a place could exist where kids were free to run, play, and learn. I longed to live on a street lined with buildings where families spent time together in the apartments above, and even when the parents were working, they were close by in the marketplace below. On Sesame Street, everyone looked out for the children. Unlike anywhere I had been, the make-believe community of people and friendly monsters valued children. I vowed to live—someday—in such a place. It was my one source of childhood faith. I wholeheartedly believed it existed and that I would live there someday.

Sesame Street was my dream, even though Wild Kingdom was my reality. From the moment they were born, the offspring on the wild plains of Africa became the hunted in a predatory world. Always opportunistic, the predators knew what to look for and waited patiently for a distracted mother. As I watched, I wondered, *Why does Marlin Perkins watch it happen? He could have saved the helpless babies from being devoured; he could have shouted at the mother or father to pay attention.* It felt too much like my own life. I imagined myself as a defenseless baby animal scoped out by various predators. *I would prefer a lion,* I decided. Death by lion would be quick. The slow suffering—ravaged limb by limb—is much worse.

CHAPTER 8

—◁○▷—

"It's Only Pokido"

A YEAR PASSED. I survived the wilderness of the neighborhood and kindergarten and began to prepare myself to venture into first grade at the public school. Once again, I was entering an entirely new environment where I would need to figure out how to blend in and, if needed, where to hide. My sister and I walked the short journey to school together. A few days a week, we were also picked up from home and taken to St. Anne's for our CCD class. By then my mom had become acquainted with other neighbors whose kids also attended, and a few parents took turns driving all of us.

Other than my constant stomach pains and a nervous condition, I quickly adapted to my new school. Daily I wished to go directly home afterward, where I could hide alone in silence and begin preparing for the next day. However, I did not have a choice. I had to go to church. Among the shortlist of things I looked forward to, going to St. Anne's after school was not one of them.

Yet, while there, inexplicably, it became my special privilege to play fetch with Father Chesterfield's big black standard poodle. He let me throw the ball for his dog without any other kids around. I didn't like the fact that his dog wasn't neutered. I had no understanding of the process of neutering a dog, but I knew our dog Yogi didn't have "those things." It was gross, and watching his dog chase down the ball made it difficult to ignore. Despite the uncomfortable visual, I did feel special because I was doing it by myself while the other kids were in class.

It wasn't long before I was required to go to confession. We had not done it in kindergarten, and I had no idea what confession was. At first, the dark and eerily claustrophobic booth with a mysterious person on the other side of the screen caused me to keep silent. However, I quickly learned we all had sins to confess. I needed to begin confessing something. From the brief teaching I'd received at church, I understood God knew all my thoughts and secrets, and it wasn't possible for me to hide anything from Him. I believed it, too. Initially, my sister became the topic of all my confessions. Whether I had or not, I confessed to calling her bad names. Occasionally I would change it by saying I hit her or had bad thoughts toward her. As time went on and I adapted to this rhythm of confessing secrets, I began feeling guilty about the secret of my grandfather's abuse. Because it was a secret, I believed it was my sin to confess. I am not sure how it came out of my mouth, but somehow I communicated what my grandfather had done.

I cannot say how much time passed between the day I found enough courage to verbalize the terrorizing account of what my grandfather had done to me and the day when a new terror arrived. It never crossed my mind that my parents should have been notified and weren't. Not much in my young life made sense. What I do know was it would not be long until I found out who was listening to my confessions. Another predator found me. My damaged soul made an easy target, and although no one else in my life seemed to notice my brokenness, Father Chesterfield had. When I confirmed it in the confessional while he hid behind the screen listening, I imagine my already broken state helped justify in his mind what soon followed.

Over the next three years, he sexually abused me. To ensure silence, he told me I was nothing and would always be nothing, declaring that no one cared about me. I am certain it wasn't hard for him to convince me that he was right. My life experiences thus far definitely supported his claims. If any doubt remained, any bit of hope that someone could help me, it didn't survive the threat of eternal suffering with the Devil. Father Chesterfield was clear: If I spoke about the things he was doing to me, I would go to hell. The concept of hell and the prospect of going there were altogether new to me. But Father Chesterfield took his time creating a vivid and terrifying image of what it is like and who the Devil was. I began having regular nightmares about hell, making damnation even more real and bringing to life the words he spoke over me.

He delivered his personal sermons to me with commanding authority, manipulating Scripture to create this lie: I deserved the unspeakable acts he performed. He read to me from the Bible, claiming false power and authority over me. From him I learned (and believed with unwavering conviction) that Satan was always waiting, and God was always watching. In this way, he ensured I would remain silent when he wasn't around to enforce it. I wasn't even sure who God was, but I knew I was afraid of Him. With its crooked priest, life-sized crucifix, and strict instructions to avoid God's wrath, St. Anne's became another house of terror for me. However possible it is for a little boy to make a commitment with himself not to tell, I did. I didn't tell anyone.

The abuse I endured from Father Chesterfield included emotional, physical, spiritual, and sexual abuse—even rape. But those words were not in my vocabulary back then, and I had no way to make sense of what was happening to me. Instead, I cried uncontrollably to my mom, pleading with her not to make me go. In the end, I still had to. The anticipation of what would happen to me consumed me. His abuse was consistent, and I knew I would face it, but I didn't know whether or not it would happen that day. This terrible expectation and the question, *Will it happen today?* became almost more unbearable than the physical abuse. The paralyzing dread of waiting for the inevitable tormented me continually.

In an effort to minimize the terror, I would tell myself, "Don't worry; it's only pokido." In a desperate repetition, I would quietly mumble the words to myself. For me, it helped to identify the trauma, which penetrated every part of my small existence. In the midst of my impossible circumstance, I needed to name it. With a name, I minimized the enormity of what was done and buried it deep within. There the rotting secrets and infectious lies would remain hidden and disconnected in my desperate attempt to survive.

While other children learned about Jesus, I sat overtaken by silent terror. Today when I recall the events, I feel a chill down my spine, triggered by the thought of Father Chesterfield's frigid hand around the back of my neck, leading me in painful silence down a hallway to the place where the abuse happened. I thought Father Chesterfield had the biggest and strongest hands I had ever seen or felt. Not ever do I recall attempting to break away from his grip. There was no place to run and no one to run to. I knew better than to yell or seek help; I was one word away from entering the gates of eternal suffering. Eventually, over the course of the abuse, I began calling him Dr. Chesterfield as a sort of explanation for what he would do. I'm not sure if it was my idea or his.

My dad was big, and he was strong. I knew if he found out what was happening, it would be the end of it. Because he had never been to St. Anne's, my dad had no way of knowing about the abuse I suffered. I needed someone to tell him. I needed someone to speak for me. Thus, I fantasized about someone speaking on my behalf. I believed someone knew what Father Chesterfield was doing to me. I believed there was a savior within the church walls—someone unknown, unseen, yet always present. That someone was my only hope.

To rationalize the delay in my rescue and to prolong some semblance of hope, I told myself whoever knew about the abuse needed to wait, for some reason, for the perfect time to notify my dad. Eventually, I believed the terrible secret couldn't remain hidden. I only needed to make it through one more day. My greatest day would be signified by the sound of a brief conversation between my mom and dad, followed by the thundering sound of our front door slamming. I constantly prayed for the slamming of our front door—a sign my dad was on his way to put an end to my suffering. The fantasy included a full confession by Father Chesterfield to my dad, a validation of the truth of what I had experienced. My fantasy ended with my dad's return to our home, where he lifted me into his arms and validated me as his son.

As each day passed, when the opportunity for a rescue slowly came and then quickly went, I reassured myself tomorrow was a new day, another chance for a miracle. Even though the spiritual abuse created a false and frightening image of God, I prayed. In my desperate place, prayer was all I had. I didn't know exactly who I was praying to, and I could not help accepting my prayers went unanswered. Regardless, I prayed for a rescuer. I held on to my hope for rescue until my final day at St. Anne's, and although a rescue didn't happen, since then I have never lost the need and desire for a savior in my life.

CHAPTER 9

―◄◦►―

Hope Deferred

LOOKING BACK, I REALIZE I was easy prey for Father Chesterfield. My parents were absent in making their presence known on the St. Anne's campus, and I carried the effects of the abuse committed by my grandfather. My only connection was to loneliness and pain. I did not even see my sister much at St. Anne's, except when we arrived together or left to go home in the same car. After a while, I did not even have those opportunities to see her because Father Chesterfield began providing my transportation, picking me up and dropping me off at home. The distance between our front door and his car, when I walked it alone, seemed like miles. I didn't know which was worse: leaving to go to St. Anne's, where at least one person knew what was happening to me, or returning home with a painful secret, wondering if some remaining piece of me could still be loved.

I was convinced something about me stood out—something telling and visible. I tried everything I could to hide it or remove it. The problem was that I didn't know what it was. I recall putting on a sweater before school one morning and noticing there was a stain in the middle of my chest. To remedy this, I cut it out with a pair of scissors. It did not occur to me that a big hole was worse. The contrast between children who have their innocence ripped from their tender souls and children who possess all the beauty God created within them is visibly clear to those who look for it.

The "it" I sought but could not find was not something tangible I could remove; it was something I had lost. I was a poster child for the abused, but no one noticed.

Some of my most difficult times were at home, where I constantly complained about stomachaches and feeling sick. The stomachaches were partially due to the fact I avoided using the bathroom. The effects of abuse are all-encompassing. It caused extensive rituals I enforced with strict adherence throughout each day in an attempt to meet basic needs, remain safe, and survive while also avoiding triggers. Going alone into the privacy of a bathroom triggered a panic I found difficult to manage as a child.

After a period of relentless complaining about my bottom hurting and crying out, "It hurts so bad," knowing I could never tell my mom what "it" was, a time came when I thought she would figure it out. *This is it,* I thought. *She will see it.* She even examined me with a flashlight. *Surely,* I thought, *the light will reveal the source of my pain.* But without any sign of concern, she simply applied ointment. Disappointment overwhelmed me. This cycle repeated itself often. Most times, my mom would do her examination without finding anything wrong. However, if I complained long enough, she would take me to the doctor. Despite my fear of the doctor, a visit provided another opportunity for diagnosing the abuse. It was heartbreaking for me when the examinations did not detect the elusive symptoms of childhood sexual abuse. Hearing the doctor ask if there was anything else, I remained silent. My mom didn't know any better, so I returned home to prepare for it to happen again. Eventually, it became too devastating for me to allow myself those brief moments of hope—only to be disappointed again.

Childlike hope is delicate. The relentless assaults began to crush my belief that things could change. Slowly, my life transitioned from hope deferred to hope given up. My childhood had ended when I was four. Because of the early trauma, I was unable to hold on to fond memories I could embrace and reflect on during difficult times. Life was simply about survival.

I do not blame my parents. Had they known, they would have rescued me. The symptoms must have been tiresome and draining for them. They had no reason to think something so terrible might have happened to me, and because of my self-loathing and fear of the Devil, I closed down any thoughts of telling them. Thus, my young life became a journey of hopelessness, and though I desperately wished my mom and dad could know, I vowed to remain silent. In the depths of my soul, I knew I was alone.

Because of this, I didn't know how to respond to normal parts of life. I cried when I heard a harsh word, whether it was directed at me or not, and physical roughness from innocent child play had the same affect. When I would crawl onto my dad's lap to play, he would get marginally aggressive with me—until I cried. It was a father's attempt to toughen me up for a world he knew firsthand had zero tolerance for crybabies. He firmly believed the world was a brutal and unforgiving place, and it was not too early to prepare for the onslaught of adulthood. I am glad I didn't know how he felt. If someone had told me life as an adult was worse than my childhood, the knowledge would have been too much.

Learning in school was impossible. Overwhelmed with the task of simply surviving, I couldn't risk preoccupying my mind with the freedom to learn. I intentionally did not seek help. The constant weight of anticipation continually distracted me, intensifying as the end of each school day approached. When the bell rang, it was the brief countdown until my return to a dreadfully terrifying and painful place. I wish I could put into words the tormenting anticipation and fear; only then could I communicate the incredible will of a child to keep a secret. If accurately told and understood, the reason I chose not to say anything would be clear. Unfortunately, there are no words.

Because I could not focus on my studies, I did not learn to read. As a result, I could not complete the elementary workbook assignments. It was my first real experience with severe anxiety over expectations separate from the actual abuse, and it triggered a fear of exposure for the shame-filled child I was. Uncovering my illiteracy would have been embarrassing, whereas the real danger was in revealing my weakness and vulnerability, which would present an opportunity for someone who was looking for the telling signs to hurt me.

What I learned in school were skills for methodically calculating ways to hide my pain and, more importantly, the effects of abuse. I made scribble lines in the blank spaces of my workbook pages, desperately hoping I could fool the teacher by the pencil markings. Adults and teachers seemed to overlook so much; I assumed the same lack of attention would apply to my assignments. However, my teacher wanted me to learn and didn't fall for my attempts at deception. As I struggled to navigate school, I noticed my classmates felt strangely free to learn. As I witnessed their progression, I could see their light growing brighter with each new discovery. By comparison, I felt myself slipping deeper into darkness.

I could not handle anticipation or disappointment, and I did my best to either avoid such situations or to create the devastation before someone else did. One Christmas, I received an inflatable Hoppity Horse toy that quickly became my favorite. I spent hours bouncing around believing I was The Lone Ranger riding his loyal horse Silver. Unlike with other toys, my interest in this one allowed for creativity, and I escaped on an imaginary adventure each time I played. Because of this, the Hoppity Horse became important to me, and I worried that it would somehow be taken away. This worry escalated until I could no longer enjoy playing with my Hoppity Horse. The anticipation of something happening to my toy became too much. I stuck it with a safety pin, deflating it before someone else had a chance to.

My actions rarely made sense to anyone, not even me. I remember my mom expressing her disbelief, knowing how much I enjoyed riding the giant rubber ball. Afterward, I did miss my Hoppity Horse, but I chose not to ask for another one. This was the first instance in what would become a pattern of self-sabotage that undermined my adult life, particularly in relationships, successes, and important beliefs intended to bring joy but holding the potential for great sorrow.

CHAPTER 10

<small>◄○►</small>

Janet's Car

CHILDREN LIKE ME, WHO suffer severe trauma, find a way, somehow, to survive. Even though they possess limited years of development and a lack of knowledge and understanding to give reason for hope, they survive. Abused children no longer possess the ability to discern a dangerous situation from one to be trusted, nor acts of evil from love. Every day and every encounter presents an unimaginable threat—one already proven real, possibly many times over. The devastating experiences instill a constant dread that intensifies until a brief and violent interruption. The momentary and twisted pause is a solitary validation of a child's deepest fear—confirmation instilled by more abuse. It proves what abused children fear is not imaginary, reinforcing their constant need to prepare for the affliction alone and in silence. Once the devastating act takes place, the worry, unworthiness, fear, and pain reinforce devastating lies, and the cycle begins all over again.

Molested children spend their silent days trying to figure out an equation too complex to solve. This desperate struggle covers the early years in a blanket of darkness. Their fragile minds race against time to figure out what is wrong. Play and rest are no reprieve. When another episode of abuse comes, the child's mind shuts down, allowing the body to surrender as it enters the violent storm. In the aftermath, the child is alone to pick up the fractured and shattered parts, with fewer remaining after each assault. The abused child lives out a frantic search for his or her clothes, hoping to cover the shame and hide the mangled pieces that will never go back to their original form. This search becomes a life-ong quest for something, anything, to cover the shame and numb the pain.

In some cases, abused children endure far more than what would drive an adult to suicide. Sadly, it is often childhood abuse—the full impact of which is not realized until adulthood—that causes many to believe suicide is the final option. Even though the physical abuse ends, for the adults abused children grow into, every other effect of the trauma remains. Years are spent developing ways to cope and even overcome in a world that generally chooses to ignore what happens to children.

Personally, I wanted to remain silent and to forget my childhood. As a man, I possessed a deep longing to be strong and to move on. I gave everything to conform to this world and its demands, only to find it filled with emptiness, lies, and deception. After a relentless search for what was promised to be enough, I discovered it never was. For me, no joy or success or relationship or possession was enough to fill the void in my soul. This was the conclusion I reached as I began my descent into alcoholism. I discovered nothing in this world could satisfy. And I could not risk facing the realities of my past in order to pursue freedom.

Of course, true freedom does exist, and it has infinite value. It also has a cost—a value measured differently for each person.

Once I met a woman named Janet. As we talked, we sensed the unspoken connection between two souls who have experienced childhood trauma. During the course of our discussion, she shared with me the abuse she had endured as a little girl at the hands of her own parents. Her story was nearly unbelievable. If it had not been for my own experience, I might not have believed her. We both had experienced abuse, yet our connection went deeper. In Janet's effort to survive, I saw my own life mirrored.

Janet, with a smile and genuine peace, calmly told me that after exhausting all other options in her attempt to forget and overcome the life she did not ask for, she arrived at the crossroads of her life. There she made the agonizing choice to be free at all costs. Freedom meant facing her biggest fear—facing the loss of the thing she valued most. This most valued possession was not a successful career or the retirement portfolio she had worked hard to accumulate. It was not about her husband of many years or even the potential of losing her relationship with her own children, whom she clearly loved.

What Janet feared most was losing her car.

She didn't explain why it was the car. She didn't need to. From an early age, she had heard her life held no value. That belief made it extremely difficult for her to value relationships, even family relationships. Ultimately, we cannot love others any more than we are capable of loving ourselves. Janet did not love herself at all. Ultimately she, like the rest of us, was created to seek out something of genuine value. The fact she was told her life had no value could not negate the intrinsically human search for value. Often, those who carry a deep void within search more intensely. I imagine Janet's car symbolized her last hope for freedom, a tangible way to escape. If she was anything like me, the prospect of losing the car, which became an embodiment of hope, meant despair. It meant suicide. With that car, she could dream about the possibility of driving off into a new life. She could disconnect from her emptiness and pain and dream that life could be different. When Janet chose freedom, she let go of what seemed to be her last lifeline.

Janet's lifeline was her car. Mine was alcohol. Though at no time did it fill the void, and in fact, it made my life worse, I feared letting it go. Letting go, to me, meant I would then have nothing.

CHAPTER 11

—◄⟨○⟩►—

Impact Management

I BEGAN PLAYING SOCCER when I was seven even though I didn't want to. I didn't want to do anything except be left alone, but my mom, noticing how withdrawn I was, believed playing soccer would help my timidity and shyness. I did everything I could to change her mind, but nothing worked. On the first day of soccer practice, I met Joe, my new coach. When I heard him speak, I became immediately terrified of him. Father Chesterfield was from Poland and spoke with an accent. Joe was from Hungary, and to my ears, the way he spoke sounded the same.

Fortunately, that was where the similarity stopped. I discovered Joe was a good man, and I am grateful he was in my life. He took exceptional care of the kids who played for him and was devoted to the team. He was loyal to those of us who committed ourselves to the game for many years. My teammates and I grew to have a deep appreciation for the sport, and through the countless practices and games, Joe passionately guided us to become skilled and competitive players. Even though he took the game seriously—which caused him frustration and massive fits of anger because his group of ten-year-olds did not play at the skill level of the Brazilian National Team—he was a humble and kind man. Joe had tremendous hope for us; he was incredibly unwavering in his expectation that each boy could be great. Occasionally, he dedicated practice time to showing movie reels of the soccer legend Pele. He would talk as if he believed we could execute at the same level.

Someone on our team nicknamed Joe "The Opossum," for the simple reason that he looked like one. I clearly saw the resemblance but didn't have the courage to call him by the name of an oversized rodent. When one of the many fearless boys on my team did, Joe would laugh, which caused me to laugh. I liked it when my teammates joked around with our coach. I loved that Joe went along with it. Though I didn't understand why, I felt a strong bond with my young teammates over my three and a half years of playing soccer. I felt my teammates knew me better than anyone, and because they came close to my damaged soul, I viewed them differently than they did me, and my observation was acceptable. More surprisingly, I loved Joe and felt terrified of him all at the same time. I am glad my mom made me play. Not only did it help with my timidity, but it helped me get through life.

Our team, the Rockwood Rockets, turned into a mini-powerhouse. We were state champions two years, and from the beginning, Joe found me a special place among the chaos of the eleven boys on our side. I was the sweeper—the last defender whose job it was to stop anyone from coming down the field and scoring a goal. I took this job seriously. I felt the weight of the world on my bony shoulders. I did not, however, quite grasp the "sweeping" part of my position and planted myself in the same spot throughout the game.

The action rarely came my way, which was fine with me. At times, I would become distracted by watching airplanes pass overhead or by picking the grass and dandelions growing within my designated perimeter. Occasionally, Joe would yell at me to pay attention to the game, which caused me to feel like I had been caught doing something bad. Immediately, I would give my best shot at acting engaged, even though the ball was at least fifty yards away. In the mid-seventies, kids played soccer on regular-sized fields. Given the expanse of a full-sized soccer field, it was possible for me to avoid having contact with the ball or players from the other team. I figured if I stayed away from the action, I couldn't mess up, and then Joe wouldn't need to yell at me.

A few years after I began playing soccer, Joe took our young team to Canada so we could compete in a soccer tournament. He had big dreams for us and was always seeking out highly competitive games for our team to play in. Sometimes he would even schedule games with opponent teams two age groups above ours. On the long drive to Canada, I quickly discovered being in a van with a bunch of free-spirited and rowdy boys was excruciating. Even more unnerving were the preplanned accommodations, which required us to be split up and housed with unknown families from the opposing Canadian team. I hated it.

All the boys were incredibly kind to me, but I was in survival mode and could not trust any situation or person. When the boy I was staying with, Wayne, invited me to play street hockey with him and his friends, I reluctantly agreed because I feared staying behind in an unfamiliar home with unfamiliar people would be worse. I told Wayne I didn't feel well and wasn't up for playing, but I reassured him I was content to watch from the sidelines. As I stood alone, watching the other boys having a great time, I felt scared and fully exposed. Consumed by these emotions, I lost control and wet my pants. My jeans were soaked, and it was obvious to all the kids. I was humiliated. It seemed Wayne sensed my shame, not only about my accident but in general, and he did his best not to draw attention to me. With compassion, he was the only one to accept my excuse— that I fell into a mud puddle.

I was six years old when Father Chesterfield began sexually abusing me. The abuse finally ended in 1974, when I reached the age of eight. After making the mistake of confessing to him about my grandfather, I decided I would never again tell anyone what had happened to me. The terrorizing fear of going to hell remained with me, along with the uneasy feeling that I was under a watchful presence. I left St. Anne's with a determination to shun church, the place I had received a deeply rooted conviction of hell and (as much as my finite mind could understand it) eternity. My young life was now missing a foundation of hope, and I did not believe the days ahead could be better. Rather, my focus was on simply surviving in silence and, at all costs, deferring certain punishment.

My ninth and tenth years marked the end of the abuse and the beginning of a new season—the lifelong process of managing the impact. For a brief period after leaving St. Anne's, I refused to let go of the dream that my mom and dad would discover what I had endured over the last five years. This is one of the many facets of God's grace for children. He allows kids to embrace whatever they need to in order to hold on, in order to hope. My need to have my parents know what I had gone through was not to seek punishment for my grandfather and Father Chesterfield; my need was greater. I wanted to explain my damaged soul. I desperately longed for them to know the cause of my struggles and weaknesses. I wished for a way to speak the shame away. I possessed a deep hole in my heart, and I wanted it to be filled by hearing my mom and dad say they were sorry it had happened through promises that I would never have to experience that level of pain again. It is hard to be a deeply wounded child and not have visible scars for show and tell.

In my final childhood attempt to create an opportunity for my parents to find my brokenness, I performed a 1970s version of a nine year old running away. I clearly indicated I was upset in front of as many family members as possible and then exited our house. I didn't travel beyond the front yard but hid behind a large fir tree and waited. With my nose about an inch away from the tree trunk, I became momentarily lost in the intricacy of the bark. I remained hidden from the view of our front door, which required little effort since nobody was actually looking for me. While I held my position, wishing for a different outcome, I stood in wonderment at the mystery of how the tiny pieces of the enormous tree all fit together perfectly. Once again, I found safety in the fir trees, a place to escape to while I anxiously waited for the sound of our front door. I wanted somebody to find me—I longed for them to discover me and carry me home. I wanted my mom and dad to sit me down and gently tell me they knew what I had been through. It was not to be.

I do not recall much relief when I realized I would not have to return to St. Anne's, although I am certain I was relieved. I do remember accepting that Father Chesterfield had escaped any discovery of his abuse against me, which meant no one would ever know what he had done. With my grandfather now unable to move from his deteriorated recliner without assistance, it seemed the end of their abuse was final. No one would ever catch them in the act. The knowledge of it would be my burden to carry alone. From that point on, I cut off all thoughts of my prior years.

Instead, I continued to find peace by climbing high into my beloved fir trees, which were scattered across my neighborhood. The massive evergreens provided a place of safety for me, a place where I could hide while keeping my eyes open to see. I used to believe that if I closed my eyes, no one could see me. Now I had found a place where no one could see me, but I could see them. Wedged between the massive trunk and a sturdy branch, I felt guarded by a gentle giant who rose far above my terrifying existence, a presence who had witnessed and known about all I had gone through. I allowed myself to believe that the wind traveling through the dense fir needles was my protector and comforter, whispering in my ear and assuring me I was safe. I did feel safe. I wanted to stay in those trees forever.

CHAPTER 12

The New Me

ONE SATURDAY, BOTH MY mom and dad came to watch my soccer game. It was a special treat, as my dad was not often able to attend. Our opponents had a player named David, who happened to be the son of a professional football player on the Dallas Cowboys; by default, this made David a local celebrity. Joe warned all of us how fast he was and instructed each of us to make sure David did not get the ball. Joe's warning made me nervous. I somehow knew I was going to be involved in the collapse of his carefully devised game plan. Midway through the game, my worst soccer nightmare began to unfold. David broke away and headed downfield, straight for me. I could hear both sidelines yelling and cheering while I stood still, hoping he would trip and fall.

Then I heard it: "Get him, Mike!"

It was my dad. As David dribbled the ball toward the sideline to go around where I stood in the middle of the field, something came over me. I started chasing after him, and as I neared, I went into a slide tackle, taking the ball and David out of bounds. Although I had not committed a foul, David hadn't seen me coming, and such an aggressive play by a ten-year-old was uncommon.

Lying on the ground, I could hear the cheers from everyone on our sideline and the protests from the other team's fans. I stood up and looked at David, who remained on the ground. For a moment,

I felt ashamed. I noticed his expression and knew what it said: "Why did you do that to me?"

My moment of empathy and attention was cut short, diverted by the undeniable pride beaming from my dad. In this decisive moment, a vision entered my mind. At last, I knew who I needed to be in my dad's eyes.

My transition into my new skin commenced immediately. I was in fifth grade in 1976, and I began to discover that if I acted a certain way, doing things that were uncharacteristic of me, it caused other kids to look at me differently. As a result, I established acceptance in a group of boys my age that I otherwise would not have associated with. These changes in me manifested most clearly in my interactions with two other kids—Jenny and Ben.

I remember Jenny as if I saw her yesterday. She was a special needs student who functioned at a high enough level to be part of my class. Initially, I was nice to her, not in a patronizing way, but simply because I was drawn to her honesty, kindness, and ability to be vulnerable. I also felt compassion for her, considering the various challenges she must have struggled with. Jenny was outgoing, and she always projected her friendly nature toward me and others, regardless of who they were. Rarely a day went by in which I did not hear the unfiltered enthusiasm of "Hi Mike!" Jenny possessed a pure innocence I admired and valued.

Jenny's physical handicap caused her to walk and run with her arm bent, as though she was constantly checking her watch to see what time it was. Some kids mimicked her by doing the same thing or yelled out after her, "What time is it, Jenny?" Because of her innocence, it was easy to engage in conversations with her to parade her limitations. One day, I joined the others in making fun of Jenny, and as I did, I sensed how terribly damaging it was.

I also experienced what it was like to be the one inflicting pain instead of receiving it. *Why did I say or do that to her?* After each incident, as I lay in bed, I would replay what I had done and ask that question until I fell asleep. Amazingly, even after I treated Jenny badly, she maintained her kindness toward me. To this day, I regret the way I treated her.

And then there was Ben. After school, the group of boys I was part of always hung out on the playground. One afternoon, in the distance, we saw Ben walking alone; he was always by himself and went out of his way to avoid speaking to anyone. Ben's appearance clearly indicated he was growing up in a difficult home, and his demeanor reflected an accepted defeat. Ben's clothes were rarely clean, and his body odor was sour. Once he spotted Ben, one of the boys in our group suggested I go beat him up. I was scared, but despite my timidity, I accepted the dare.

I ran toward Ben, feeling weaker as I got closer to him, even though I knew he didn't see me coming. I jumped him from behind, knocked him to the ground, and began punching the back of his head. Ben lay there, surrendering to my attack without trying to defend himself. When I had inflicted enough pain, I stood up, and Ben slowly got up too. With his hair matted in grass and dirt, Ben turned and looked at me. Then, without saying a word, he continued his walk home. In his eyes, I saw myself.

To this day, despite all the shameful things I later did as an adult, these two events rank among the worst moments of my life. I had started down a terrible path. Fortunately, this misguided diversion ended.

During my eleventh year, my life suddenly changed again. Unexpectedly, something happened that caused my life (almost) to start all over. I thought my prayers had finally been answered in 1977. Though the events didn't quite follow my fantasized script from earlier years, for me, it was close enough.

One day, I developed a stomachache of epic proportions. It was noticeably severe and gave measurable pain to my silent suffering. It was so bad that I didn't have to embellish it. All I could manage to do for over a week was lay in a fetal position on the couch and moan, but I refused to cry. Somehow, I knew this pain was special. I was open to relief, yet I rejected any treatment threatening to cure the source before a diagnosis could accurately measure my affliction. Finally, the diagnosis came.

I always knew something was wrong with me—a rottenness most could not see but that evil somehow sensed. It became clear, I was seriously sick, and my mom, who had eventually gotten her driver's license, drove me to the emergency room.

"His appendix ruptured," the doctor said, his words punctuated by a glorious look of concern. I heard him explain to my mom how I needed to have emergency surgery to remove it. *I don't know what an appendix is, but I am glad I have one that ruptured.* This was terrific news, I thought to myself.

After surgery, the doctor explained to me, I had waited too long before coming to the hospital, and an infection had set in. In order to drain the fluid, he needed to insert a surgical tube into my stomach. I did not bother trying to explain to the doctor the infection was there long before my appendix burst. I was intentionally careful about filtering what I said, not wanting to alter his focus and momentum. I knew he was on the right track. What drained from the tube and onto the gauze pad resembled the hospital tapioca pudding, and the smell was similar to the main course. The doctor may not have diagnosed my past abuse, but he found out what was wrong with me. He identified the rotten core of who I believed I was—in addition to the infection caused by a deep wound—neither of which ever healed.

The fluid from my ruptured appendix took weeks to drain. With each changing of the gauze pad, I saw further evidence that whatever was rotting inside me was coming out. After the doctor determined that the fluid had drained completely, it was time to remove the surgical tube. Unfortunately, the skin around the tubing had healed, cinching tightly around the elastic. It was a slow and painful process to remove it. The doctor pulled and the tube stretched, causing severe pain, not to mention the added visual effect, which was much worse. I experienced a strange sense of joy through the multiple trips back to the doctor's office during the extraction process. Nonetheless, I was glad when the tube finally came out.

The long-awaited diagnosis had authenticated my agony, the treatment was administered with care, and I had convinced myself I would be separated from perceived weakness, and I would not allow myself to be disappointed by a missed diagnosis.

After the surgery to remove my appendix, my parents seemed to have a new appreciation for me as a son. Now with most of my childhood erased, it appeared I was not alone in my desire to forget the past. No one in my family wanted to remember or even reflect on the earlier years. When they brought me home from the hospital, it felt like it was for the first time, like my life was about to begin as an eleven-year-old boy.

CHAPTER 13

◄◊►

The Good Life

FOR SOME REASON, THE appendicitis, surgery, and brief scare over my wellness meant something to my mom and dad. I embraced the attention and held on to every moment, hoping it would eventually reach the deep void in me.

The best part of this change was that my dad began spending time with me. Our father-son time together was always an adventure. We spent every weekend hunting and fishing, and even when my dad went with his friends, who either didn't have kids or chose not to bring them, my dad always took me along. During this time, I felt loved by my dad. He became my real-life hero.

One of our favorite places to go was on the Deschutes River in Oregon. My dad purchased a jet boat specifically made for going through white water rapids, and I enjoyed everything about it. He was larger than life to me when he stood at the wheel, always confident and in complete control. I marveled at how he fearlessly maneuvered the boat between huge boulders and through the raging waters. From what I remembered of my earlier years, my dad possessed little patience for my timid and fumbling ways, but something had changed in how he responded to me. He patiently taught me how to fish, and even though it was easy to snag, and I lost a lot of his gear, he genuinely didn't seem to mind. We went on a trip every weekend, and while I still attended the local grade school, I would run home as fast as I could on Fridays, knowing my dad had the boat and all our camping gear loaded up and ready to go. It was an exciting time for me, and I fondly remember rounding the last corner of the last block to see him waiting in the driveway for me. For the first time, life was good.

I also loved bird hunting with my dad in Eastern Oregon's high desert. Because I had spent much of my time hanging out with the neighborhood fir trees, I treasured nature's abundance. When exploring the outdoors, I appreciated the beauty and continually wondered at how all the pieces fit perfectly together. When I closed my eyes and savored the sweet smell of juniper trees, which thrived in the dry climate, I felt lost in peaceful joy.

When we were hunting, I was always cautious and aware of where I stood in relation to my dad. When a bird flew by, I did all I could to avoid getting caught in the line of fire. I felt I needed to be extra careful. If I was standing in a massive crowd of people, and someone shot an arrow straight up into the air, I believed it would inevitably hit me. It wouldn't matter where I ran or where I hid, wherever I ended up standing would be where the arrow would hit. Life had shown me I was an easy target.

One afternoon, we walked for miles in the midday sun while hunting. Because the heat was wearing on us both, my dad decided we would stop and rest behind a grouping of sagebrush and wait for unsuspecting doves to fly by. The birds were fast and agile flyers, and if my dad was going to get a good shot, he had to be alert. Immediately after we stopped, three doves darted through the air directly in front of us, and my dad opened fire with his shotgun. The loud blasts always made me cower, but I tolerated the noise because I enjoyed everything else. From where I stood, I could see he had hit one.

In the midst of my excitement, without telling my dad, I circled around outside his line of vision to retrieve the bird. I arrived where I thought it had collided with the ground, and as I turned to look in a different direction, the dove jumped. My dad shot again, and the spray of BBs peppered my flesh. Luckily, I was far enough away that the buckshot only penetrated my skin. Even more fortunate was the clear evidence of my wounds. My white shirt made it seem much worse than it was. When I looked down at my chest and saw the blood, I instinctively dropped to the ground. Strangely, I didn't feel scared, and it didn't hurt. Most strangely of all, I didn't cry. Without hesitation, my dad rushed to me. When he dropped his gun and sprinted toward me with a look of deep concern on his face, he made me the happiest kid on earth.

The blood provided the evidence of my injury, releasing me from the burden of carrying another invisible wound. The past abuse left me with no margin, no capacity to take on additional pain in silence. I always felt like I was at my tipping point, like I was constantly risking falling deeper into despair—a place I might not return from. When I got hurt in a visible way, it felt different from the secret pain and shame. In some ways, it was freeing, and I welcomed it.

My dad lifted me in his arms and ran in the sweltering heat. I was his only concern. Gently, he put me in the front seat of his truck, reassuring me I would be okay. We raced to the small town hospital, and after a quick examination, the doctor told us it wasn't serious. I received an injection in my chest to numb the area so he could remove one BB near my heart, where the doctor thought it could cause problems. The rest, he left. These remaining BBs lived in my skin as reminders of one of my greatest days. Over the next few months, the BBs worked their way to the surface of my skin, where I picked them out with great pleasure.

After my quick recovery, our dad-and-son adventures continued, and we headed for the Deschutes River at the peak of Oregon's bone-chilling rainy season. My dad's friend, Jerry, and our black lab, Howe, came along. Jerry and my dad were excited to catch winter steelhead, I was excited to be with my dad, and Howe, well, he was just excited.

The river was high and seemed to be flowing particularly fiercely. Because of our frequent summer trips, I had learned the water flow patterns of each rapid and the course we needed to take. During the dry season, with decreased water levels, exposed rocks clearly marked our path. However, on this trip, none of the rapids looked the same. The powerful force of the high water generated by heavy rain echoed throughout the canyon. The unfamiliar sound caused my stomach to tighten with fear and my breathing to become shallow. The dark sky and thundering river seemed much bigger than all of us, even my dad.

The unwavering consistency of my dad's routine on the river provided me with a needed sense of control. There were specific spots we fished, as well as sets of rapids upriver and downriver that my dad had decided were off limits. Even though the rain was constant, and it was cold, we still had a great day of fishing. As evening began to settle into the canyon, we cruised upriver to our final fishing hole. However, due to the high water level, my dad failed to recognize a rapid chute that we had decided to avoid. Mistakenly, he committed the boat and the four of us into the middle of the large waves and churning currents.

My dad respected the strength of the river and understood the boats limitations. Here, the jet boat's motor lacked the horsepower to push through the opposing current, and we were stuck in the clutches of an overpowering force incapable of caring whether we lived or died. Unable to move forward and unwilling to risk certain doom by going backward, we were suspended, and slowly the boat began to sink. All my dad could do was to shift the boat to the side, keeping the bow facing upriver. Though we were nearly submerged, he was able to maneuver the boat with great skill and composure in the midst of uncertainty to the safety of the shoreline.

The experience brought on a familiar and unlikely combination—anxiety and the satisfying thrill of danger. I always expected something bad to happen, but I could not foresee when or in what form it would strike. But if I could control the circumstances of danger, I would choose pain over the anticipation of unknown pain every time, especially if my dad was near while I experienced it.

By the time we reached the shore, it was getting dark, and we needed to return to our campsite. After bailing water out of the boat, we hopped in and headed downriver. No one spoke. I'm sure my dad and Jerry reflected on what could have been a disastrous outcome. My thoughts centered only on the awesomeness of my dad.

We approached the last rapid before camp, and as he always did, my dad drove up to the throat, picked his course, and circled around to enter. When the boat is at low throttle, the water will guide it to where it needs to go between two large boulders. Once aligned, full throttle is engaged to give the boat the power and ability to navigate within the narrow channel. It always went like clockwork, and I would list the necessary actions quietly to myself as my dad performed them. However, when I said, "Full throttle," nothing happened. I saw my dad press the lever forward like usual, but instead of hearing the motor scream, I only heard a brief sputter. Immediately, the force of the water drove the aluminum boat right into one of the large boulders and tipped it sideways. The three of us went overboard. Due to his low center of gravity, Howe miraculously stayed on board.

As we were tossed into the frigid water, my dad grabbed my life jacket with his powerful hand. I knew he would not let go. Our eyes connected—his assuring me I was safe. He then instructed me to kick off my hip waders. If I kept them on, they would fill with water, acting like an anchor and pulling me to the bottom of the river. Fortunately, we were all wearing life jackets. Still, the water was moving fast, and we had little control over where it would take us.

Howe, on the other hand, was about to embark on his own adventure. Dogs have the enviable ability to believe all of life's events, both good and bad, work together for good. I am convinced there is nothing in this world that they worry about. Given Howe's situation, his belief in all things good was in fact a good thing. The throttle, which moments before had misfired, suddenly sparked and accelerated to full speed. The boat took off downriver with Howe as the only passenger.

With the water's unrelenting force at our backs, slamming my dad and me into large boulders, I watched Howe assume his position at the bow of the boat. He seemed oblivious to the reality that no one was driving the boat. It traveled about a quarter mile down river, turned, and started heading back upriver toward us. The jet boat was barreling down on our location, but before it reached us, it hit another large rock and changed direction. Howe was now on a collision course with an island, and why he continued to hold his position at the bow was beyond me. The battered boat, traveling at full speed, crashed directly into the rugged shoreline and launched completely out of the water and into the trees. The outboard motor, still firing at full speed, created an eerie screeching sound, enhancing the already spectacular chaos taking place in the dark and remote canyon.

Finally, the engine seized as we floated by the crash site. I could see Howe's head rising up happily from the side of the boat. While my attention was on the boat, my dad focused on getting us to shore safely. His powerful fist never let go of me while he fought the swift current with his other hand, trying to direct us to the side of the river that our campsite was on. The force of the river's current wouldn't allow it. It pushed us to the opposite shoreline, the uninhabited side with open rangeland, steep canyon walls, and railroad tracks that followed the contour of the riverbank. By the time my dad pulled himself and me out of the river and onto the rocky bank, the sun had already set, and the temperature continued to drop. Confronted with an exhausting and bitterly cold walk in either direction, he contemplated our next move while he caught his breath. During the late 1970s, not many people fished the river in winter, and we knew we were alone. We hadn't seen any other campsites or anglers the entire day.

Jerry got separated from us when we entered the water. He ended up traveling farther downstream, finally pulling himself from the thrashing, cold water onto the shores of Buzzard Island. For some reason, all the buzzards in Max Canyon return to this island each evening to spend the night, perching high in the trees. If it was me, I don't think I could have handled that many emblems of death staring down at me as if I was a future carcass, and I would have closed my eyes and jumped back in the river, hoping for a better outcome.

Calm and unafraid, I looked up at my dad and said, "Even now, I would much rather be here with you than at school." I'm sure he believed I was trying to make him feel better. The truth was that I was comparing my cold uncertain future while in his presence to my lonely past, and I really did mean what I said. When I was with my dad, it was not possible for fear to overtake me.

My dad decided a train was our best option. The trains hauled cargo up and down the tracks regularly. We had watched them go by while we fished during the day, and I had listened to them pass through the night. My dad's instructions were clear; we would wait for a train, and then he would wave it down as it approached. While we waited for the silence to be broken, I sat close to my dad, his arms wrapped around me, trying to keep me warm.

Before long, the unmistakable sound of a freight train vibrated the ground and shook the massive rock structures shaping the expansive canyon.

"Stay put," my dad told me.

He scaled the large and slippery rocks to the railway and stood in the middle of the tracks. Once he determined which direction the train was coming from, he faced the train and waited. It was a spectacular site. The engine light illuminated his imposing figure, and as I watched, I honestly believed my dad was strong enough to hold out his hand and stop it in its tracks. As soon as the engineer saw my dad, the horn exploded into the night.

Within a safe distance, knowing he had been seen, my dad stepped off the tracks. The mighty locomotive passed, and I heard the brakes engage. I could not believe the train was actually stopping for us. Always rigid in my thoughts, I hadn't allowed myself to think beyond my dad's idea—as far as whether or not it was realistic. I refused to contemplate an actual rescue because avoiding disappointment was a critical part of my survival. Further, I could not comprehend why something so big and powerful, carrying expensive cargo surely exceeding my value, would bother to stop in the middle of nowhere, disrupting its determined course, to help the two of us—maybe for my dad, but certainly not for me.

The train seemed to extend forever as I watched it slow to a crawl. The cars inched past my dad and me until the train came to a grinding halt. The engineer had skillfully timed his stop so the caboose came to a halt directly in front of us.

Using the train's radio, the engineer contacted the two men in the caboose, who were busy assisting my dad and me: "How many are in the caboose? Are they injured? Are there any others involved in the accident?"

My dad told the men we were okay, but his friend was on an island downriver, directly across from where the conductor sat in the locomotive. Later, we found out the engineer exited the train and yelled out to Jerry, letting him know he could fire a rope across the river and pull him to our location. Jerry's options were to reenter the water in darkness and be dragged through turbulent water or to wait for a river rescue the next day.

"I am not getting back in the water. I will take my chances spending the night with the vultures." Jerry's position was clear.

There was no question. I was having a blast, and my experience in the caboose only made it better. A wood stove filled the caboose with a warm smoky haze and pleasant smells. I felt like I was in a scene from an old western. Riding in a train was a new experience for me, and as I shared the memorable journey with my dad, I wished it could go on forever. The men in the caboose listened intently to my dad's account of our story. I listened too, mesmerized by our adventure so much so that I forgot I was a main character. The two men seemed to enjoy becoming a part of our adventure and playing a significant role in the rescue.

The nearest town was The Dalles, located in Oregon's scenic Columbia River Gorge, fifty miles from our current location. The train altered its scheduled destination to take us there. It's hard to say how many people were involved or, at a minimum, affected by the decision to help my dad and me. We were cared for, far back in the caboose, and could not see or hear the decisions made on our behalf. Reflecting on the rescue, I am amazed and moved by their actions, which proved our safety and well-being outweighed the inconvenience, consequences, and cost to all those affected by the engineer's choice to stop. The moment the man who was driving the train saw my dad standing in the middle of the railroad tracks, he engaged the brakes. He would not have had time to contact anyone to get permission. He simply saw a man in need and responded.

When we arrived in The Dalles, the town's sheriff, who was aware of our pending arrival, greeted us at the train station. Just when I thought our adventure could not get any more exciting, a patrol car arrived and escorted my dad and me to the small town police station. When we arrived, we found a dry set of county-issued prisoner clothes hung in the locker room for us to change into—my dad's clothes were too small, and mine were too big. The sheriff offered me a tour of the small holding jail, and I looked at my dad, who gave me a nod.

"Yes, please," I enthusiastically answered and jumped at the opportunity. I felt safe walking beside the sheriff, with his thick black belt, holster, and gun. It was an incredible feeling knowing, with every assurance, no one could touch me. *I wish the sheriff could walk beside me throughout my life,* I thought. I would be able to face every moment without fear. I would be able to breathe. I was tired of holding my breath every time I felt threatened, and I knew under the covering of a powerful protector, life would be different.

The next morning, the sheriff drove my dad and me back to the town of Maupin. Located along the Deschutes River, the small town is essentially a staging area for all the recreational activities taking place on the river. Although crashes are not common, they happen enough that an entrepreneur could make a small business out of retrieving crashed or sunken boats from the unforgiving water. Thankfully, we didn't need to discuss the additional service of recovering a body, even though we did have to pay extra to retrieve Jerry from Buzzard Island. As for Howe, he was not injured and seemed to enjoy his evening alone, which included dining on an entire box of Ding Dongs—foil and all. Howe's adventure did end well, just as he had expected.

CHAPTER 14

---◄○►---

Hello Grace

IT WAS A GRATIFYING season. I was able to block out the earlier events of my childhood, and life improved for me. I loved spending time with my dad, even though being with him always carried an element of risk. In the end, all our mishaps only enhanced the memorable times we spent together, which included overcoming adversity. I began to understand I couldn't get a free pass from life's challenges because my dad was with me, but his presence did mean I could face adversity.

My dad continued to include me in almost everything he did, and even though I became increasingly skilled at blocking out the issues connected to my past abuse in order to enjoy my time with him, many of my struggles remained. A constant and relentlessly condemning voice spoke to me about my worthlessness. When my dad was not around, fear overpowered me, and as I got older, the paralyzing grip of shame began to squeeze tighter.

I also possessed a biological alarm that struck every day at three o'clock. Every day at that exact time, it sent my body a clear signal to shut down regardless of what I was doing or where I was. The years of abuse at St. Anne's had programmed my mind to expect that abuse was going to happen. Three o'clock was the time when I had prepared my body and mind to enter a world filled with loneliness, darkness, and pain. Throughout my teenage years and even as an adult, when the critical hour hit, I would retreat into silence and fear. Today there are still times when I have to remind myself that I do not have to go anywhere.

Even though my life improved outwardly, my hidden struggles continued, creating a constant tension and effectively strengthening my will power. The ability to force a detachment from the painful memories provided a season apart from the underlying source of the pain, though the pain itself remained. The burden of a nagging affliction became normal. I accepted it as if it was a birth defect. For me, this thought process was necessary for survival, but at the same time, it was dangerous. Over the next six years, I entered a transformation process built upon a fractured foundation of trauma and lies. Given the compromised groundwork of my new starting point, there was zero chance it would support my longing to build a normal life.

In my desire to create a new and normal life for myself, I applied myself to school, learning enough to advance to each grade. In an attempt to remain unseen, I always stayed out of trouble. Adapting in a constantly changing environment was always a struggle. Nothing I did maintained a direct connection to an intentional outcome. In my mind, two plus two did not always equal four, and everything was a trick question. Survival was complex, to say the least. The way my mind worked, I was constantly thinking things like, *If I stand here, maybe I will end up over there. If I say this, maybe the person will hear my intentions. If I look like this, maybe I will not be seen.* I rigidly obeyed the rules and showed the utmost respect for teachers, but not because I was simply good-natured. My only goals were to avoid pain, hide the secrets of my past, and most importantly, disguise who I really was.

In 1979, despite my best efforts, somebody took notice of me in seventh grade. The unwanted attention was not a result of applying myself in class or achieving exceptional grades. It wasn't from following the rules or breaking them, and it wasn't because of my developing ability as a soccer player, which was, for the most part, unknown. From all I could gather, someone became aware of what I believed I had hidden so well. Having somebody notice me always made me nervous.

Each year the seventh grade science teacher, Mr. Smith, selected a few students to go on a field trip, making his selections based on who he felt displayed a strong interest in the subject. He picked me. I did not know I was interested in science. Mr. Smith held an afterschool meeting for the parents of the students who were participating. My dad attended with me, and Mr. Smith took considerable time calmly explaining, in surprising detail, how he noticed my reluctance to participate in class. He said he believed it was not from a lack of interest or desire.

As I watched Mr. Smith discuss the specifics with my dad, I felt weird, almost as if the direct communication was a boundary not to be crossed. I knew Mr. Smith was in authority over me while I was at school, and my dad was the rest of the time, and the two were not supposed to cross paths. Mr. Smith went on to say that it would be helpful for me to be a part of the field trip, as if he put considerable thought and preparation into his presentation to my dad. It almost seemed like my science teacher engaged in a one-sided argument on my behalf, trying to convince my dad that my involvement might help me overcome some of my fears related to learning and that science provided exciting opportunities for learning.

Both of us "kind of" listened to Mr. Smith, and when he was finished talking, my dad looked at me, allowing me the opportunity to decide for myself. My dad didn't question me about why I was fearful in the classroom, and up to the meeting with Mr. Smith, I didn't know why no one had asked. My painfully quiet demeanor was how my parents saw me; it defined who I was.

"No, thank you, Mr. Smith, but I appreciate the offer," I said, declining his invitation. I never actually considered going on the field trip, although part of me wanted to. I was too scared. After I thanked Mr. Smith for the opportunity, I wished to explain how much I appreciated his genuine interest in me. I wanted to ask him not to give up on me, but unless I shared all the pieces to my fractured story, I knew my request would not have made sense.

Looking back, I wonder how Mr. Smith was able to see me when many others could not. The ability to see beyond the surface is not common. How did he know I—who sat quietly in the far corner of the classroom, motionless at my desk, disciplined to avoid questions and give answers—was afraid? Mr. Smith was correct, not only about the fear but also about my interest in science. I did want to learn. Unfortunately, I still believed I was behind in my development. I had already determined what my future would look like based on the lies others had spoken over me. I believed I was nothing and would always be nothing; science had no power to prove otherwise.

Yet my seventh grade science teacher saw me through different eyes. Somehow, he knew my behavior was not who I was called to be. Because his invitation to go on the special trip was not one I earned by works or performance, Mr. Smith offered me a gift I did not deserve. I did not even know what grace was at the time, but through Mr. Smith's simple acknowledgment of me, he allowed me to experience it. For me, this isolated attempt to understand my struggle while in the midst of prolonged brokenness became a hallmark in my life. For the first time, an encounter with grace penetrated the fear-enforced barriers surrounding my soul. It did something I thought was impossible.

CHAPTER 15

◀◦▶

Keeping the Secret

THEN, THE SUMMER BEFORE I started eighth grade, my family moved to the country. I was nervous, not because I liked my old neighborhood and school, but because I had figured out a system and routine that kept me safe. Now I had to start all over, finding a safe way to hide at a new school. However, I was excited about living in the country. Before long, my black lab, Maggie, and I began going on daily adventures. We lived on ten acres, with much more forestland surrounding our property, and the two of us explored it all. Maggie had been with me for about three years by the time we moved, and she was my best friend.

Although I preferred spending time with Maggie, I was able to make a few friends at my new school, and midway through my eighth grade year, I invited two of them to spend the night. I cannot say why exactly I thought it would be a good idea to risk compromising my protective bubble through altering my rigid routine of isolation. From previous conversations the three of us had, I knew I was far more naive than they were on many levels, but I also sensed I had experienced more darkness than they hopefully ever would.

After my parents went to bed, one of the boys asked if we had any alcohol in our house.

"Yes, do you guys want me to go get a bottle?" I answered.

I knew my mom and dad stored a few liquor bottles in the cabinet, and wanting to impress my new friends, I willingly offered it. My parents drank on occasion—socially—but I do not recall ever seeing them drunk.

I grabbed a bottle of vodka and took it upstairs. I had tried beer before but felt it weakened my defenses in concealing the hidden shame. My previous experiments with alcohol had led me down an unwanted path, bringing me face-to-face with a past I had vowed to stop thinking about. However, this time was different. The three of us started drinking straight from the bottle. My friends took small sips, struggling to get the straight alcohol down. However, once I took a drink, I could not stop. I drank until the bottle was gone, and I was drunk. The affects were immediate. I quickly lost control of the tightly guarded image I had worked hard to create.

During the process of becoming intoxicated, I crossed an internal barrier, an off-limits place I had promised myself I would never enter. After an initial and brief moment of euphoria, a moment I was going to recall, I started to cry and could not stop. Unfortunately for all of us, it was the ugly version—the hideously embarrassing kind of sobbing only alcohol can evoke. I said to my friends, who I am sure were seriously reevaluating the friendship at this stage of the sleepover, "Maggie doesn't love me." My dog even sat in a state of awkwardness, looking at me as if I was crazy. It was awful. I knew Maggie did love me, and the humiliation of what I had done in front of my new friends was devastating. I declared I would never drink again.

The alcohol exposed something in me no one was ever supposed to see: I truly believed I was unlovable. This belief and rejection was so deep it even encompassed the affection of my loyal dog.

Yet even amidst the humiliation, I felt momentary relief and a tangible release. Somewhere between the first drink and my loss of control, the stronghold of my grandfather and the demoralizing grip of Father Chesterfield had weakened. The booze gave me the ability to finally break free and run; it also gave me something to run to. I thought, *This is what it must have been like for the children on the kindergarten playground.* It was a tainted glimpse of freedom, a promise of a way out. Thus, as the embarrassment of my emotional breakdown faded, my memory of the momentary freedom I experienced strengthened.

I walked through my high school years lost and virtually dead inside. Although I continued to play soccer with my club team, in 1980—my freshman year—I quit the high school team. After an uncomfortable encounter showering with the other players, during which a teammate peed on me, I was done. It was obviously gross, and though I could understand the disgusting locker room humor, I felt like crying. I said to myself, *The other boys can see it; they know, especially the one who peed on me.* Immediately, I became scared. I knew better than to show it, so I casually stepped out of the shower, got dressed, and rushed home. Running away was the only option to manage my fear. Soccer practice started at three o'clock, right after school, and I was not able to turn off my internal alarm. Even before the peeing incident, it had proven too difficult to play the game I loved in a paralyzed condition.

One day, as I was walking home after school, I saw my dad standing outside of our house, looking like he had something important to talk to me about. My mind raced. He was rarely home early in the day, and I could not think of a pending need for punishment. A quick review of my latest activities brought nothing to mind, yet I felt nervous and guilty anyway. As I got closer, I saw he was actually excited.

"Hey, I have something to show you," my dad said. He was having trouble containing his joy, which was both strange and uncomfortable for me. His behavior was unfamiliar. He rushed to open the garage door, revealing a 1969 Chevy Chevelle. The car was in perfect and original condition. My dad stood tall, beaming with fatherly pride; he clearly loved being able to give me this car. I, on the other hand, was in shock. I didn't know how to react. Because I had learned, over the years, to keep my emotions under tight control,

I rarely showed excitement about anything. However, I did the best I could to express my appreciation.

My dad walked around the vehicle and opened the driver's side door, inviting me to take a seat in my new car. It was definitely a classic, and all my friends and classmates would surely be envious. All of a sudden, my nervousness began to escalate. Easing into the driver's seat and grabbing the steering wheel, the vintage smell of an old vehicle consumed me. It was not the smell of neglect, cigarettes, moisture, or fast food stuffed under the seats. The car was well cared for. It smelled exactly like Father Chesterfield's old station wagon.

My dad could tell something was wrong. "Thank you, Dad. I can't believe you got this for me. I really like it." My attempt to show gratitude fell short. What I told my dad was a lie. I desperately didn't want to hurt his feelings. He was excited. I am sure he wished his dad would have bought him a car just like it. I felt conflicted, but I knew I could not keep it. Over the next few days, I worked up the courage to tell him. I did not consider telling him the truth, but I needed to tell him something.

"I don't like it! I was afraid to tell you," I said.

In silent pain, I rejected a gift I knew was special and appeared ungrateful. It was one thing to despise myself, but sensing my dad's great disappointment in me was devastating.

When my grandfather had passed away a few years before, I told my parents I was unable to attend the funeral. Without emotion, I briefly explained I had homework to do. I saw anger in my dad's eyes and waited for the verbal lashing, knowing I could not explain. "My dad is dead, and all you can think about is yourself," my dad said.

To my dad, the situation with the car was a continuation of my insensitivity and inability to express gratitude or consider the feelings of others. It is a miserable existence living a lie in order to keep a secret.

I hoped that the more distance and time I put between my life and the experiences with my grandfather and Father Chesterfield, the less impact they would have. Unfortunately, the effects of the abuse began to resurface and take their toll. As I entered my senior year of high school in 1984, I became depressed. My mom could tell I was becoming increasingly withdrawn, and my words confirmed it: "I don't want to live anymore."

She asked if I would be willing to see a counselor. Tired of the hopelessness, I said I was willing to try. But when I entered the therapist's office, I felt my tongue press against the roof of my mouth and my jaw clench down. Refusing to say a single word, I sensed the counselor's frustration with my lack of effort to help him help me. I actually looked forward to the appointment, secretly hoping the counselor would see my pain and uncover my story without me having to say anything, but he could not. *I wish someone could know what happened to me; but then again, I don't want anyone to know,* I thought to myself.

Both my mom and I left the appointment feeling disappointed, but my private time with the counselor remained off-limits for discussion. Deep down, I remembered the confessional, and I vowed I would not make the same mistake again.

CHAPTER 16

—◄○►—

No More Religion

THE ONE THING I enjoyed was soccer. I eventually decided to play for my high school team again, despite my locker room fears, and I created an elaborate strategy to help me avoid the showers. By my senior year, I was team captain. I also made First Team All-State, was voted the US Army's Athlete of the Year, and was inducted into my high school's Hall of Fame. I am embarrassed to admit it, but my classmates gave me the dubious award for "Best Appearance." The award gives a strong indication of the extent I went to hide my shame. At the final high school assembly, a staff member announced that I had received a full-ride soccer scholarship to a Christian college.

I didn't like the fact it was a Christian school, but I figured it wouldn't really affect me. In my mind, the school's religious focus had no relevance. Clearly my recruitment was for my athletic abilities and not for my knowledge of theology or my low SAT score. After St. Anne's, I had determined to evade church, and I was not going to open a Bible either. Believing I would not have to do either, I accepted the offer.

Practice and preseason games started about a month before school, and I was doing well. The coach named me the starting sweeper as an incoming freshman, which came with a level of respect from others and demanded a level of confidence from me. While most of the players lived on the college campus, I lived at home, which allowed me the opportunity to go home and shower after practice. The fear of being naked and showering in front of others was still extremely difficult for me. I believed my nakedness would somehow expose the horror of my past and reveal the shameful secret of who I was.

As the beginning of the fall semester neared, I submitted my class schedule. In choosing courses, I scanned for descriptions indicating a prerequisite of little intelligence, a small work load, and no testing. Based on what I was reading, I couldn't make a determination, only finding classes related to Bible study or with religious-sounding names. Out of necessity, I convinced myself the course requirements were not required after all, but were really electives for those who believed in God. I believed in soccer, and an education wasn't part of the plan, particularly in religion. Studying the catalogue, I did my best to select course titles missing references to the Bible or theology, which left few options.

But as it turned out, it wasn't quite that easy. Prior to classes starting, an administrator contacted me. "Mike, I noticed you neglected to sign up for Bible Study. Would you like me to add it to your schedule? It is required."

How am I going to get out of this? I thought. Initially I resisted, but eventually I shifted my position to pacify the friendly woman from admissions who was probably confused as to why I had applied to a Christian college in the first place. It was official. My registration confirmed my enrollment in Bible Study 101, but I had no intentions of attending.

Fall semester began, and I went to my classes—with the exception of Bible Study. Aside from the fact that I was skipping the class altogether, anticipating someone would eventually notice, I felt like life was going well. I made it two weeks before Barry, the school's head soccer coach, approached me.

"Why aren't you attending Bible Study?" he asked, adding, "I have also been notified that you are not attending chapel."

I told him the truth about chapel, explaining I hadn't been aware it was mandatory, even though I noticed my teammates going. I honestly assumed it was their choice and they wanted to. There was an awkward silence between Barry and me. He fully expected a valid reason from me, but I gave him nothing. I had nothing to give. Eventually, Barry patted me on the shoulder, making it clear that if I wanted to continue playing on the team, I was required to attend chapel and Bible Study.

Without notice, I dropped out of school and quit the team. After a couple of days of me not showing up for practice or classes, I received a call.

"Where have you been?" Barry asked.

Again, I chose to lie.

"Are you willing to come down to my office and discuss this?" he asked.

I agreed. My dad came along. We both sat in front of Barry's desk while he asked why I wanted to quit. Before I could answer, the coach said, "I really had no idea you were having problems; everything seemed to be going well for you." I don't think Barry believed I was actually going to quit so early in the season. He assumed whatever was bothering me must be a misunderstanding, and whatever was my concern, there would be an easy fix with his help. I only needed to let Barry know what it was.

I stayed silent.

"He simply doesn't want to play soccer or attend college," my dad said, breaking the momentary silence. What he said on my behalf was not true. I did want to do both. But in my mind, there was no other option.

Understandably, Barry was shocked. While looking directly into my eyes, he asked if it was my final decision.

Beginning to cry, I shook my head yes. I couldn't look him in the eyes. People could look into my eyes, but I found it impossible to return a confident reflection. Because wise men often determine character in another man this way, I would always fail the honesty test—though my dishonesty was not for the reasons they assumed.

My dad was a building contractor and a master carpenter, and after I quit college, my dad offered me a temporary job working for him. The job was contingent on me making an effort to decide what I wanted to do with my life. My parents didn't express a desire for me to go to college, and they were indifferent about my decision to quit. However, my dad was clear in our agreement. I needed to find a job separate from working with him. It was time for me to become a responsible man. At eighteen years of age, life's benchmark made sense to me.

I loved being with my dad every day, and I felt safe working for him. I was awed at his knowledge of the trade as well as his skill and strength. He could lift large quantities of lumber and walk along narrow walls standing two stories above the ground without any hesitation. I watched in admiration as he took lightning fast measurements, cut the wood perfectly, placed it, and then drove nails in with a single swing of his hammer. He appeared to do it all in one fluid motion. The sweet smell of sawdust covering the job site reminded me of when I was a little boy, and my dad would come home from work with his white t-shirt coated in the tiny particles. I enjoyed all aspects of the job site—the smell of freshly milled lumber, the sawdust, the sound of skill saws and hammers, and most of all, my dad's presence.

Unfortunately, I was terrible at all things related to construction. I struggled with the skill set my dad was highly proficient in. My attempts to drive a nail, even with a swing count exceeding my daily wages, were feeble at best, and the nail, appearing to be made of rubber, would bend before it had a chance to make contact with the other piece of wood. My timid use of a skill saw left a cut displaying a series of "S" turns. I would hand off the ordered cut, both too short and too long, only to have it tossed into the scrap pile. I could not effectively carry more than two pieces of lumber on level ground, let alone a narrowly framed vertical wall standing twenty feet high.

I was terrified of heights, and once positioned on top of a wall, I couldn't stand without freezing. Patience and compassion for a fragile young man who lacked the necessary skills and, therefore, disrupted the rapid workflow was not a part of the hard-driving construction industry. My dad and I quickly realized this was not my calling, not even on a temporary basis.

To help me out, my dad contacted a friend who owned a successful business, also within the construction industry, and inquired about a possible job for me. The owner, John, was in his late twenties at the time and was hard-working, focused, and determined to succeed. He was driven. I often heard my dad and others who knew him say he was wise beyond his years when it came to business. He commanded a strong work ethic from the many he employed and had a reputation for a hot temper. None of these qualities or character defects caused me too much concern. I had previously met him, through my dad, and immediately took a liking to him. The one thing I heard about my potential new boss that put me on guard was his extreme religion. In fact, rumors went around that he was a bit of a wacko when it came to Jesus. I was concerned. I did not want to see this side of any man, let alone someone who held authority over me.

Despite my fears, I accepted a job as a laborer in the lowest level company position possible. As a result, I didn't have much contact with John. But through occasional opportunities to talk with him and my observations of him, I began to develop an admiration for John. The thought of him being religious remained in the back of my mind, and on some level, I expected to witness the hypocrisy and manipulation I knew well. Yet as we talked and I began to know more about John, I was drawn further into how secure and confidently grounded he was in a truth I didn't know. Slowly, my admiration for him grew, not because of his abilities and status as a business owner, but because of something else, something about John that I could not quite identify.

As far as I can remember, John didn't speak directly to me about God or try to force a belief on me. What he did communicate was his unashamed relationship with Jesus. He placed more value on this one truth and defended it with more conviction than anything else I had ever witnessed a person do. John's uncompromising stand seemed to provide him a powerful shield of unwavering confidence against the relentless threats from competitors, organizations, and individuals who fully intended to take him down. In the midst of both incredible success and intense pressure—at times when others in similar positions surrendered their faith to the daily battles and temptations—John did not.

John chose not to waste his efforts hiding his imperfections from me. He was not interested in pretending to be anything other than who he believed God had created him to be. As I watched him, I longed to live the same way. I didn't want to be him, but I did want to have the same freedom he enjoyed. However, I was unwilling to accept what John believed about this freedom—authentic freedom could only be found through Jesus. I had already rejected all religious paths, and I was determined to find another way while possessing exactly the same protection, freedom, and favor he possessed.

In this way, a seed for freedom dwelled in my heart. The one obstacle I believed stood in my way would one day become the living truth that would save my life.

CHAPTER 17

---◄○►---

Sweaty Socks

ONE FRIDAY AFTER WORK, I received a call from Tim, a friend whom I had played soccer with for many years. He called to let me know that he and his family were moving to Santa Rosa, California. Tim planned to attend the junior college and try out for the soccer team. He asked if I was interested in doing the same. If I was, I needed to decide quickly because they were leaving in less than a week. Not only would Tim be there, but also some of our old teammates were already playing on the junior college team. It didn't take long for me to decide. Although I felt nervous about my decision, I was going.

Before I arrived, I arranged to move into a house with two of my old Oregon teammates, as well as a few future Canadian players who had migrated down from the north. I liked Santa Rosa right away, and having a few of my old friends around helped me adjust to my uncharacteristically bold move.

The refrigerator revealed my new teammates' main food group—beer—and by the looks of the packed shelves and drawers, they had big appetites. Perhaps alcohol was why they were extremely funny in a relaxed and welcoming kind of way and always had me laughing. I liked them immediately. My discernment regarding my new roommates was validated when I discovered they had adopted a house dog. Molson received his name after the Canadian beer and for good reason. When introduced to Molson, he didn't bother to get up to greet me or anyone else but remained motionless in his relaxed position on the couch, choosing not to exert himself. Molson laid on his back, proudly exposing his enlarged belly, which clearly reflected his thirst for the same beverage he was labeled by.

I began practicing with the soccer team and secured my spot as the starting sweeper. I maintained my rigid routines in a new environment and denied tendencies to relax my efforts to reinforce them. Every move I made was both calculated and subtle in my desperate attempt to keep from being exposed. Exhaustively methodical, I controlled my environment, and the rigidity of my routine left no margin for compromise. I lived close to the campus and avoided showering in the locker room after practice, while at the same time, I tried to create the illusion that I took showers all the time in the locker room. My anxiety levels always escalated toward the end of practice as I began to formulate my plan to avoid the locker room and showers. Drawn from a painstaking skill set that I grew to depend on over the years, the irrational behavior was draining, but like many things, it became normal.

Fall semester was set to begin within a few weeks, and I nervously opened the catalogue of courses to select my classes. To ease my primary concern, I first made sure there were no religious courses. I was relieved when I could not discover even one.

The night before my first day of classes, in my second attempt at college, we held a party at our house, and I proceeded to get thoroughly drunk. My drinking during this time was still contained to weekends and social occasions. After the incident with vodka in eighth grade, I always made sure to avoid drinking myself into a scene of defamation and exposure. It was a constant concern. Each time I picked up a beer or a glass of hard alcohol, I could feel the buried pain aching for release. But at times, I took a calculated risk of exposure in order to step into a momentary feeling of freedom. When I found the distilled happiness, I held on to it for as long as I could. Even then, I knew sadness lurked at the bottom of the bottle. Still, it was the best that I had found, and it was worth the price.

Though I was having a great time at our party along with everyone else, later in the evening, I felt drawn to walk over to the campus, where I sat down in the grass directly in front of the school's brick monument. Knowing I was alone, I began to cry. *I am not going to fail this time.* I was starting over, it was 1986, and my new life in California was going to be different. It was a new beginning.

Amazingly, my adjustment into my new life began to provide an opportunity I didn't feel I deserved while also revealing abilities I was unaware I had. The school environment and learning remained difficult, yet I felt a strong sense of belonging, which fostered my growing capacity to overcome. Privately, I spent more time than my friends and classmates on homework in an attempt to conceal the hidden shame of being a slow learner. For the same reason, I also opposed study groups and seeking assistance from the professors. If I did, I was certain I risked exposing my limitations related to learning.

Then I enrolled in a required English course. One of our assignments allowed us the freedom to write a short story on any topic we wanted. Feeling unqualified to write a paper, I was relieved to hear it only needed to be a short story. In class, we finished reading William Faulkner's *As I Lay Dying.* The dark novel, written in 1930, covers the journey of a poor and dysfunctional Southern family who sets out to bury their dead matriarch, dragging her corpse and coffin cross-country. I was fascinated by the way the stench of the rotting remains horrified and caused misfortune to whomever crossed paths with the coffin and each family member. This family, before their journey, lived in isolation, wallowing in the normalcy of their own sickness. They saw absolutely nothing wrong with their behavior. Yet when the entire clan set out on their ignorant and destructive trek, they were a virtual traveling circus of sin, and each fully expected the outside world to be the same. This was the first book I had ever read. I was nineteen years old.

For my paper, I wrote about a pair of soccer socks I had banned from the washing machine because I thought they were good luck.

In my mind, washing my socks meant I risked losing whatever it was they possessed and therefore losing my ability to play the game I enjoyed. Like the rotting corpse, my socks certainly possessed the scent of decay, and yet I was unwilling to wash them. When I slipped them on and stepped onto the field, I felt transformed into someone else. I wrote about how I struggled in everything I did until the day I put on my special socks. However, once I removed them, placing the soiled and sweat-soaked socks in my athletic bag, I returned to darkness. I described in graphic detail how badly the socks stank and the nauseating effect the pungent odor had on those who encountered my gym bag and me. I tried my best to put into words what I honestly believed—concluding whoever became close to me would somehow suffer a loss in one form or another. Those socks became a topic I found easy to chronicle.

I'm sure if I still had the paper and read it today, it would not be as good as I like to remember. But there is no doubt, the assignment influenced my confidence and growth. When I got the graded paper back from my professor, I saw she wrote a large letter A with a circle around it, which I took for emphasis. She also wrote, "I loved your story! You are creative." I don't know if she was generous with her grading and freely handed out compliments, but the grade and those kind words transformed me. For the first time in my life, I believed I was smart. From this point of discovery, I approached learning with a new confidence and perspective.

In addition to school and soccer, I began working a part-time job in the campus distribution center. I delivered packages to the various departments and enjoyed getting to know the students and staff I visited regularly on my route. The added responsibility made me feel a part of something. I also became close to my boss, Lee, who was in his late sixties. On the surface, he appeared to be a grumpy old man. However, for reasons I didn't understand, he and I got along great. On occasion, he would even take me along on his weekend fishing trips.

The president's office was one of my regular distribution stops, and often I would take a little extra time to visit with a girl who worked as an assistant to the college president. Eventually, I overcame my fear of asking Stacey out, and we began dating. Quickly, I learned she did not approach relationships casually. When she invited me to meet her parents, I was reluctant, yet I found myself only a few days later driving to their house for dinner. Stacey greeted me at the door, clearly feeling no need to mask her excitement. Enthusiastically, she introduced me to her mom and dad, who were genuinely interested in meeting me. "Nice to meet you, Mike! We have heard so much about you," Stacey's parents said, immediately putting me at ease. I quickly gathered that it was not a common occurrence for them to meet their daughter's boyfriends simply because there had only been a few, but clearly it was normal for them to be involved in Stacey's life.

They seemed like kind and loving people, but I could not overcome the small crucifix hanging on the wall in the living room and the Bible strategically placed on the coffee table. *How is it possible that I wasn't able to notice Stacey's religious upbringing?* I questioned myself. Immediately, the evening was over for me. I was unable to get beyond my discomfort and remained shut down the entire visit. I left as soon as it was appropriate.

Despite her parents' troubling religion, I liked Stacey, and she didn't seem to notice my discomfort in meeting her parents, so we continued dating. After a few months, she initiated a talk about our relationship.

"Where do you think our relationship is going, Mike?" she asked.

Why did she have to ask me that question? How am I going to tell her our relationship will soon be over? I wondered.

My long silent pauses weren't bothersome to Stacey, and she broke the silence by telling me that she was a virgin and was saving herself for marriage and her future husband. I was relieved. I immediately assured her I respected her decision, and it would not affect our relationship in any way. Although my primary thoughts were self-centered, I did feel drawn to honor her choice, and I am glad she was able to receive my response as such.

However, the truth was, after she told me, I felt a deep disgust about myself. It was another proof that I was dirty and deeply damaged. It didn't matter that I had no choice. The conviction I felt about myself was both certain and confusing. I knew men were not supposed to feel this way about themselves or about sex, but there was no doubt that I did. Aside from the self-hatred swirling around in my head, I also experienced relief. It was a premeditated fact that our relationship would end, not because of who she was but because of who I was. I knew our time together would soon be over, even before she shared her vow of celibacy with me. For me, experiencing intimacy with someone was impossible, and the potential burden lifted through knowing I would not have to worry about the complications of sex in our relationship. It was my privilege to understand who she was through her honesty; it was her misfortune to experience deception through my secret.

I placed no value on sex, and the few times I had encountered it, I felt nausea, shame, and a permanent disconnect from the person I engaged in the relationship with. I believed my opportunity to learn and my ability to experience the treasure of true and loving intimacy was crushed during my innocent years. What remained was a shameful disrespect for a selfish and hurtful act.

From the first time I met Stacey, I could tell she was different. She possessed a certain confidence and expectation for good things in her life. I recognized her right away. Stacey was just like one of the kids from my kindergarten playground. She was one of the children who would run, laugh, and play with abandoned freedom. Stacey knew and trusted God's love as well as her parent's love. She held the special knowledge of her true value. Stacey was treasured, and it was easy to see. My relationship with Stacey lasted over a year—the longest I would spend with one woman until my first marriage.

CHAPTER 18

>—◄◦►—

Fear Management

My time in Santa Rosa marked a special season in my life and helped define the improved man I wanted to become. When I graduated with my associate's degree, it was with academic honors and as a First Team All-American Scholar Athlete. This was at the junior college level, but I could not have been more pleased.

Even though events in my life began to exceed my expectations far beyond anything I thought possible, I continued to wake up each morning with piercing terror. During sleep, my defenses relaxed enough to allow fear to seep in and occupy my emptiness. The first few minutes after awakening always involved a tremendous fight to regain control and bury the past all over again. By this time in my life, I expected this morning struggle. Because of this, I found it difficult to close my eyes and fall asleep at night. I was afraid of the morning. Because I developed a deep appreciation for my new life, I began to feel I had gained more to lose. I feared the happiness I discovered was in jeopardy and fear would be victorious once again.

I wanted to continue my education and life at Santa Rosa Junior College and wished it was a four-year university. It felt like home to me. Although I rejected opportunities to connect with professors, I certainly bonded with my friends, teammates, soccer coach, and the people I worked for on campus. I didn't know it at the time, but as my final year was ending, Butch, my soccer coach, sent my transcripts to the admissions department at Cal Poly in San Luis Obispo, California. Butch was also in contact with the Mustangs' soccer coach, arranging an offer for me to be on the team. Not long after, he informed me of my acceptance into Cal Poly's business school and gave me the details for the school's soccer team—should I choose to accept it.

"Thank you, Butch; I had no idea you were doing this for me," I said. With both sadness and great appreciation, I accepted. I liked my coach. He was quiet and unassuming. At first glance, Butch didn't appear to have insight beyond the soccer field and a winning season, but I was wrong. My coach possessed vision far beyond and was able to see much more, including me. He appreciated who I was, and I should have been able to notice more about him. Prior to my last season, Butch handed me the captain's armband to represent our team in the coming season, and he always went out of his way to make sure I was doing okay. When he secretly sent off my transcripts for me, it became apparent that he wanted to do what he could to make sure I would be okay after I moved on.

San Luis Obispo was the most beautiful place I had ever seen. I had grown to love Santa Rosa and the people there, but Cal Poly was more than I deserved. The campus seemed big and intimidating compared to the tight-knit community I had recently left behind. I was starting over again, but this time was different from all the others. I was not moving on from a place of hurt, disappointment, sadness, and failure but from a place of belonging and encouragement, and in the midst of it all, I was moving toward who I wanted to be. This made my transition much more difficult.

I moved down the summer of 1988 before fall semester and began to train with the soccer team. I was taken in by and, at the same time, felt uncomfortable about the amazing things happening in my life. With unfamiliar feelings flooding my mind, I unwillingly fell into paralyzing fear. It didn't matter that I was twenty-two years old; when I heard my new coach, Franz, speak with his German accent, I felt as afraid as the seven-year-old boy who had heard Joe speak for the first time.

Nevertheless, I trained, practiced, and played in preseason games and earned the starting sweeper spot. My heart was not committed, but I continued to play anyway. With school about to begin, a wave of self-doubt came over me, specifically related to the belief that I could continue to learn. *You are not going to be able to do both and need to quite the soccer team,* I told myself. The fear of failing academically quickly overtook the shaky confidence I had developed, and as a result, I decided to devote all my time and energy to school and the job I received in the college's admissions office. I notified Franz that I was going to quit. This decision was not entirely based on my doubt about my capacity to continue learning, but was also influenced by the nagging worry about showering in the men's locker room and the exhausting routine I would have to follow in order to avoid it. I didn't want the added stress of figuring out and maintaining a completely new system in an unfamiliar and much larger environment. It was all too much. As I grew older, the fear, shame, and anxiety related to showering with other men increased, and I could not overcome it.

Franz responded in anger, trying to get me to change my mind. The fact I had decided to quit early in the season meant he had wasted a valuable spot on the team on a quitter. Yet my decision was final. As I walked out the door of his office, I knew Franz was one more person, on a growing list, who had crossed paths with me and my smelly gym bag.

For me, it was another missed opportunity. Not playing soccer was difficult for me because I loved the game. I had worked hard and had overcome so much to get to where I was. Now I missed the camaraderie and friendships I had developed through playing a team sport. I wondered how I would do, not having the ability to escape my life by putting on my socks and stepping onto the field. Playing soccer had been the one constant in my life and the only thing I was ever passionate about doing. The game allowed me to persevere in many ways. Ultimately, I didn't think I deserved it.

I settled into a routine of going to class and work while making a few friends. I enjoyed the friendships I developed, but something was still missing—the definitive bond between teammates formed through competitive sports, particularly those who started out together at a young age. I tried finding similar relationships through clubs and other organized activities, but close friendships remained unavailable. I even joined a fraternity, but quickly rejected the initiation process during a dark ceremony resembling an exorcism.

I lived in a house with five other roommates, two of whom were engineering majors and thrill seekers. This combination enabled them to invent devices feeding their appetite for adventure. One of their brilliant ideas was a homemade bungee jumping contraption. Their momentary inspiration quickly moved into the production phase, followed by an even quicker execution and field-testing. My roommates hauled their cords and harness to a remote bridge high up in one of the surrounding canyons. The span of the concrete structure was relatively short, but the shear depth, carved out by the river below, appeared bottomless. The bridge selected as the jump site, due to the remoteness and low traffic volume, was perfect for the illegal jumps. As an added measure of caution, my roommates jumped at night.

Confronted with the misfortune of receiving an invitation to go along with my roommates, I reluctantly concluded that I had no choice but to accept. Fortunately, if there was anything fortunate about it, my offer came after several months of testing the equipment. But then again, I started to wonder whether they could have possibly worn the cords to the point that my weight would cause them to snap. I was nervous and scared but refused to let them see it. My trepidation would have been reasonable if based on the reality I would soon be standing in darkness, perched high on the ledge of a remote bridge three hundred feet above a shallow, boulder-laden stream. Being tied to a low-budget makeshift apparatus put together by a couple of twenty-two-year-old pot-smoking textbook engineers who spent less time on the project than they did cramming for an exam should have frightened me. But my despair was stirred by a more terrifying and distant ordeal.

Fearfully anticipating an overpowering loss of control while riding in a car and driven to a place of secrecy was nauseatingly familiar to me. Stepping off a ledge and experiencing a freefall into darkness was not much different from what I had experienced when I took the first timid step out my front door each day as a kid. I remained sober, motionless, and silent in the back seat as we made the drive—all the while trembling like the frightened boy I once was. My body shook the entire way, and I worried I was going to pee my pants.

One of my bodacious Southern Californian roommates, Dan, went first. Displaying absolute adventurousness in his jump, he showed no hesitation as he leaped headfirst. It was actually fun for him, and I marveled at the fact he wasn't showing off or trying to prove anything; he was just clinically insane.

Dan was smart, but he prohibited his mind from getting in the way of his fun. My previous outing with him should have given me a pass on the bungee jumping, but there was a part of me that liked the fact my roommates enjoyed trying to get me out of my comfort zone. Dan's dad was an airline pilot for American Airlines, which probably explained why a twenty-two-year-old college student without a job had his own plane. When Dan invited me to go flying with him, I jumped at the opportunity, picturing us flying in style aboard something along the lines of a Learjet. I was still at the age where I believed that making $150,000 a year could buy a man anything he or his son wanted.

When Dan and I arrived at the San Luis Obispo airport hangar where he kept his plane, I could not believe my eyes. For a moment, I wondered whether he had built the plane at the same time he and his buddies had built the bungee jumping contraption. After we taxied onto the runway, while Dan was preparing for takeoff, I asked, "Is it an illusion, or is that really duct tape on the wing?" He confidently confirmed my observation. Thankfully, duct tape and all, we made it back to the ground safely.

As I waited for my turn to jump, standing about a foot from the edge of the bridge, the trembling increased throughout my entire body. There was no turning back. *If I die, I hope its quick and painless,* I thought. When my idea of a misadventure came, my roommates helped me slip on the harness and gave me an overview of what to expect. They then asked me a series of questions, but my jaw had already clenched shut, and I could not get a word out. I stepped to the ledge, looked down into absolute darkness, and then jumped. The blind freefall provided the same uncertainty I encountered each day when I entered a world I could not control. I knew danger lurked. I fully expected it to strike with devastating speed, but I was incapable of accurately surveying my surroundings.

Bungee jumping, when it is pitch black, provides no point of reference. It is impossible to tell if you are in a freefall or are ascending from the recoil of the cords. The only time I knew what stage of the nightmare I was in was when my lower intestine pressed against my Adam's apple at the peak of the accent. Then I dropped into another tailspin.

I survived the jump and declined another invitation to do it again. It was such a bad experience, I no longer cared if they knew I was afraid.

CHAPTER 19

-◄O►-

Home Again

AFTER GRADUATING FROM CAL Poly, I returned to Oregon, moved in with my parents, and began searching for a job. I scheduled interviews with a few CPA firms but already knew I disliked accounting. If I had learned anything in earning my accounting degree, it was that I did not want to be one. I chose accounting because, on some level, it satisfied my underlying need to have everything add up. Even if not everything added up, in accounting, the problem could still be reconciled. Unmindful of the principal at the time, it was what kept me engrossed in the subject, but it didn't mean I wanted to do it for the rest of my life.

I enjoyed the construction industry and wanted a career keeping me connected to the job site, where I could be involved with building something tangible. During my summer breaks while in college, I would return to Oregon and work for John as a laborer on his projects. I was not adverse to hard physical labor and actually preferred digging ditches to accounting. Maybe it wasn't that I liked using a shovel as much as it was an opportunity to spend time talking with John. However, I needed a longer-term plan and decided to find my way into the industry from a different angle. There was no question that I lacked the ability to develop actual construction skills, but I was not going to let my construction defects stop me. I figured I could run the business side.

In 1991, without a business plan or much thought to future implications, I asked my dad if he would let me become a partner in his small, custom home building company. Before he could answer, I told him that he only needed to pay me what he could afford and promised to take over the accounting, which I knew he despised. Not having to do the books was not going to be enough incentive for my dad, so I added a more tangible value he could really appreciate. "I will even clean the job sites," I told him. Cleaning out the houses and picking up the scrap piles was perfectly fine with me. I wanted to be on site, and I didn't care how I got there. My dad reluctantly agreed, adding it was a bad idea to mix family and business. I should have known my dad was correct from the beginning, given my family could not even mix as a family.

In this second attempt at working with my dad, I quickly learned that I was no longer the child who needed his protection, and he was not the paragon of perfection and strength I had unfairly held him up to be. Although I wanted him to remain the blameless, self-reliant, all-powerful, and all-knowing man I marveled at as a child, I would soon discover he was not. My dad could not be. The difficult truth is, no such man exists.

My dad and I were business partners from 1991 to 1998, and we experienced more success than failures working together. I believe we made a good team, and I remained in awe over his knowledge of the trades. Eventually we separated, and I started a separate company, but we continued to work together, with my dad acting as the general contractor on my projects.

Five years had passed since I left home for college, and it was clear nothing had changed. I gradually felt myself slipping back into the skin of the ten-year-old boy I once was, trying to communicate to my parents without saying a word, trying to get them to see something was terribly wrong.

Eventually I purchased my first house, where I quickly learned to enjoy my independence. I was determined not to slip into the despair of my past, and I was committed to avoiding the pitfalls I had witnessed at home. Little did I know, despite my declaration that failure was not an option, my calculated plan was miserably flawed. My target was not to repeat the mistakes made by my parents, and as a result, all I focused on were mistakes. Unaware of what truth was or even where to look for it, I accepted my parents' beliefs and normalized them in my daily thoughts. I assumed the entire world held the same set of lies and perspectives. I thought that I just needed to try harder than my mom and dad at living them successfully. Yet after I achieved each goal, added another asset to my balance sheet, and won the favor of those I envied, I still felt like I was pushing freedom farther away.

Because I was painfully shy and deathly awkward, I rarely dated. Thus it was on a blind date that I met my first wife, who would become the mother of our son Cole. She was nineteen years old, and I was twenty-six, but we didn't see any issue with the difference in age. Without our awareness, both of us had become stuck in our emotional development as children and remained trapped within the limitations of a survival mindset, making our ages irrelevant. We felt fortunate to have found each other; our powerful connection was both immediate and unidentifiable.

Within a year of meeting, I proposed, and we married shortly afterward. Blinded by our commonality in pain and a magnetic deception, partnered with the absence of truth and healing, my ex-wife hid the secrets of her past in an attempt to move on in life. Like me, she did this without malice and in hopes of a better future. Like me, she operated her life according to a rigid instructional manual that taught her how to bury the pain, forget the past, move on, and (most importantly) never tell her secrets. It is amazing how widely distributed those instructions are and how many of us follow them as if our lives depended on it.

My wife and I married six years prior to Cole's birth, in 1999. Shortly after his birth, I received an invitation to attend the wedding of one of my close friends in California, who had been a classmate in Santa Rosa. I looked forward to reconnecting with Bill and was particularly excited to have my newborn son come along on the trip. I was so proud of Cole, and yet it scared me to love him. We arrived at the church a few minutes late, and when I pulled up to the front entrance, I became paralyzed. I suggested my wife take Cole in and find us a seat while I parked the car. I averted joining them inside. Overwhelmed with anxiety, I drove around until the ceremony ended, picking up Cole and his mom at the curb. Not surprisingly, she asked what had happened. I answered with a lie, saying I could not find a place to park. Recovery from such paralyzing times of fear was unthinkable. I wanted to go directly home and isolate. Thus, a trip I had looked forward to ended in disappointment, fear, and a deeper disconnect from the hope that I could find a life beyond the memories of abuse. For years after the discouraging event, I had no contact with Bill, figuring it was of no use to maintain a friendship.

When Cole was only eighteen months old, his mom and I divorced. I was afraid to be a dad and figured my only beneficial contribution to raising my son was through providing for him financially. My short-minded view made me obsess over the details of my work, and I made sure to disguise my worry as a form of self-sacrifice. The more determination I summoned, the more withdrawn and absent I was at home, and after a period of neglecting my family, I received a phone call from my soon-to-be ex-wife. I listened quietly as she calmly told me that the moving van was in our driveway, and she was leaving me and taking our son with her.

Our life together, leading up to this call, was full of good intentions—absent of the often irreparable damage caused by hurtful words, violent emotional or physical attacks, failed counseling, or discussions regarding divorce. Individually, we had experienced varying degrees of those situations in one form or another, but they had happened long before we knew each other, and because we were unhealed, we carried them into our marriage.

Even though I was not the one who made the call, I recognized what was happening. It was an immediate disconnect, a predetermined belief that the marriage would end. There was an underlying need to start over before the inevitable abandonment and anticipated pain arrived—all of it triggered by the silence and lies we used to protect secrets neither one of us wanted to keep. We were both effective at filling in the blanks created by silence with the unimaginable answers—answers already proven real by our previous life experiences.

Our marriage officially ended in 2001, and both the rejection and loss were powerful enough to strike at a place deep within me, rendering my once effective coping mechanisms ineffective. Throughout my life, I went to great lengths to avoid pain and was skilled at protecting myself emotionally from relationships and situations threatening to reach the unhealed wounds caused by past abuse. However, the divorce and the pain of my separation from Cole penetrated my defenses with ease and collided with all the fears and suffering I had determined to suppress. It opened the floodgates to my painful secrets. This event marked the beginning of an uprooting journey I would not willingly chose for myself—a journey so painful I would not have believed it possible to survive if given a glimpse into what it would entail before it began.

This event led me to seek out psychotherapy with Dr. Claremont, which eventually led me to the day when I opened a newspaper with a headline describing my hidden shame.

CHAPTER 20

Meet Me at the Bar

While sitting at the bar, as I read the rest of the story written in 2002, summarizing the alleged sexual abuse committed by five priests, my body remained motionless. I was shocked to discover the same horror I had experienced may have happened to other boys who were now men, and at least one was willing to talk about it publicly. I thought about how this man's claims applied to my own life. What would happen if I were willing to air my secret shame like the man in the article? I knew it involved tremendous risk. The priest was a proclaimed man of God, as evidenced by his robe, title, and good works. If he was guilty of the crime, he certainly would be unwilling to confess the secret of his sins. The other man, the accuser, if he was telling the truth, was not a credible person by comparison, as documented by his own sinful life.

I thought about the label of unspoken disgust that brands a fully-grown man assailed with bad choices who decides to make a graphic claim of sexual abuse. It only elevates the perception of some underlying weakness, filth, and suspicion in the victim when there is a disclosure of rape, even though the man was a child when the crime took place. This is not my observation as a victim; it is truth. I'm not sure why, but I'm sure it contributes to why few victims come forward to tell their stories. When the silence is finally broken, words lack the capacity to express the devastation and loss.

Because no visible scars, no DNA, no witnesses, and no confessions are available—but only the passing of time—doubt often remains.

Drinking more whiskey, I thought about what I had read. For the first time, I felt validated. I expected the article to name Father Chesterfield and St. Anne's, but there were other names instead. The article went on to describe how the male accuser claimed his hope had perished as a direct result of the sexual abuse and trauma. "I've lived a life separated from God; I've lost faith. Alcoholism. Drug addiction. If I would have come forward, no one would have believed me," the man in the article said. He was thirty-seven years old, roughly the same age as me, and after years of rigorous rituals to help us forget, vows of silence, countless attempts to overcome, hopeless desperation, and coping mechanisms, we both appeared to be discovering at the same time that it had all stopped working. What remained were haunting memories and an inability to heal.

By this time in my life, my head only functioned as a storeroom for detached thoughts, experiences, and emotions. I methodically processed everything through a restrictive funnel, providing my conscious mind with only the information I needed to survive. Yet I processed the news article differently. The brief account of two lives—a priest and a boy—made sense to me, and I began to experience a subtle shift. Part of the shift meant that I was no longer willing to remain silent. I called Dusty and asked if she would meet me at another bar closer to home.

"I have something important to talk to you about," I told her.

Dusty agreed to meet, and as I anticipated breaking my silence for the first time since sitting in a dark confessional as a frightened six-year-old boy, I felt an overwhelming sense of peace. My mind quieted, I caught my breath, and the rapid pace of the world slowed.

When she arrived, we sat down together, and I jumped right in.

"Did you read today's paper?" I asked.

"Yes," she said, curious to know what was going on.

I was surprised, but I wasn't nervous. After a brief pause, I told her my life experiences were similar to those of the man in the article.

Dusty and I had always shared an unspoken connection and unidentifiable commonality between us, even though we appeared different in many ways. As I told her my story, she listened quietly, and her loving presence assured me that she understood the painful secret I had held on to for so long. She didn't question why I hadn't told anyone as a child or why I decided to tell her then. I was surprised when she told me, after she first read the article, although unable to explain why, she somehow had known there was a connection to me.

Dusty allowed me to share all I was able to piece together in the dark booth at the bar. Then, after a silent pause, she began to share with me a painful secret that she also had carried throughout her life. For the first time, Dusty shared her buried secret.

As if she was still a four-year-old girl—the tears running down her cheeks, reflecting the true source of pain no one else was allowed to see, she said, "I was sexually abused as a child, too." For Dusty, the physical attacks had ended nearly two decades prior, but the lies and emotional affliction remained. The passing of time couldn't diminish the hurt or erase the condemning voice in her head. As a grown woman, Dusty took ownership of the heavy burden simply because she hadn't screamed and she hadn't run. However, what the child knew—and the adult Dusty forgot—was that no one was listening, and there was nowhere to run.

As a child, Dusty believed the destructive words spoken over her within seconds of the first violation. Her loving expectations were shattered by terrorizing fear and feelings of worthlessness. The innocent and carefree little girl who shined brightly was gone. Dusty's soul turned dark, and she went silent. Just as I became the shy and timid boy, Dusty turned into the independent girl. At a young age, with her declaration made, she accepted that she was alone in her secret, and no one could ever help. From this point forward, the abuse, trauma, and lies infected every one of her life experiences and influenced every decision she made.

When innocence is taken and all seems lost, a child who has suffered trauma will find something to hold on to in order to survive another day. For me, it started with believing my dad would save me and ended with finding safety and comfort high up in the giant fir trees. For Dusty, it was her older brother Johnny. It only took the one time for Johnny to pick up Dusty up from the house where the abuse occurred for her to hold on to the belief that he would be the one to rescue her. She held on to the hope that once Johnny, who was ten years older than her, arrived, he would lift her in his arms and carry her home. Her big brother's presence would deliver her from the pit of a dark and cold basement. He held his embrace the night he carried his little sister home, and in the safety of his arms, Dusty prepared to enter another house, wondering whether there was still a part of her to be loved. She wondered because there was no assurance—only silence.

Dusty loved her mom and dad and still does. Like my parents, they determinedly believed the past was the past and needed to remain forgotten. Alcohol was their temporary and effective means of keeping the painful memories buried. It was likely neither Dusty's mom nor dad knew the source and depth of each other's pain, even after decades of marriage. The booze provided her dad with the ability to maintain the illusion of a successful man who sacrificed to provide for the family. It facilitated her mom's steadfast efforts at maintaining a storybook image of a woman giving tirelessly to her four kids, making sure they had everything they wanted. Her parents earned the respect and admiration from all who knew them. However, like all facades, without a foundation of truth and healing, cracks appear, and without exception, it all crumbles. Social status and materialism cannot support the compounding weight they create when used to bury a wounded heart. Instead, if the burden does not crush the current generation, it passes down to the next, until one day it does.

As Dusty told her story, she too embarked on a journey from which it would no longer be possible to turn back. On the same day, in the same place, together, we both courageously allowed a small ray of light to shine on our darkest secrets. Come what may, our journey through both pain and liberation toward true identity and the gift of freedom began.

CHAPTER 21

―◄O►―

Breaking Silence

I BELIEVED THAT, IN breaking my silence, somehow the longings of my childhood commanded a form of justice and a realization of my deepest desires. The confession, validation, and explanation of why life was hard for me would sweep through my past, present, and future, making it all okay. Even though much of my life had passed by in silence, I hoped to finally be validated and to discover who I was for the first time. I truly thought that since I had broken my silence, the path to freedom would be level and straight. I expected someone would be willing and able to grab my hand and walk alongside me while I picked up the pieces of my shattered life and help me finally catch up to where the world expected me to be. It didn't happen the way I had hoped.

Until then, I had spent life living a lie. It consumed most of my thoughts. With great effort, I had meticulously created the details of a false identity. I was certain the man I had become was not who I was meant to be, but the thought of unwinding my adult years was overwhelming. Despite my best efforts at remaining disconnected, my lies raveled throughout the lives of others. People made important decisions based on who they thought I was, and I felt responsible to maintain the façade to protect them from the consequences of who I believed I was. For years, I made decisions with specific and broad implications. I entered into agreements based on trust by communicating persuasive intelligence, all of it based on fear. Thinking about the burden I had created for myself through the responsibility and obligations I had to others due to their reliance and belief in the person they thought they knew was overwhelming. There were times when I believed it would be easier to continue living the lies, thinking maybe the lies were not lies after all. I tried to convince myself I could block out the pain and overcome, once again, the familiar adversity I faced. I did not believe the adversary could be confronted. I did not know my enemy had already been defeated.

Even though the pain persisted, there were times when I truly thought I had arrived and could continue down the same familiar path. I accumulated the necessary proof to show I was someone, and by all accounts, most people believed it. Yet I wanted freedom desperately. I discovered truth cannot partner with lies, and if I wanted to keep living the lies, they would keep me imprisoned as the days, months, and years passed. To understand this was one thing; what to do about it was another. Life was rapidly passing me by. I had a son, a business, financial obligations, and a false identity I painstakingly protected. Time wouldn't pause while I tried to undue all I had done, and at the same time bring current a life that should have been. My window of opportunity for a rescue by my dad had passed. It was no longer possible for him to pick me up and hold me in his arms, speaking words of affirmation and assurance.

I believed I could not tell my parents what was happening to me when I was a child, but I could now as an adult. I always wondered what they would have done back then, and I wondered what they would do now. So I told my mom and dad what had happened with my grandfather and Father Chesterfield. I do not know what I expected them to say or do, but what they did do was go silent. They didn't say a word.

Their silence angered me, and I decided to do for myself what I desperately wanted someone to do for me when I was a frightened boy. Alone, I would confront the one responsible. Had my grandfather been alive, I would have started with him. I wondered if Father Chesterfield was even alive after so many years. If he was, I was not going to rely on anyone else. I would face him myself.

I fueled my drive with alcohol, glorifying my self-destructive mission to stand face-to-face with the man who had robbed me of my innocence. As I planned and visualized how it would all go down, I drank and drank and drank. From the moment I woke up in the morning until I passed out at night, I drank. Throughout the day, I would consume an average of twenty-four beers capped off with a pint of vodka. I no longer cared what people thought of me, which before was the only thing I was ever capable of caring about.

I was still in contact with my friend, John, whom I had worked for as a teenager. When he heard about my excessive drinking, he suggested we meet. When we did, I shared with him my past, the demons I continued to battle, and the hope I wished for but couldn't find. I liked talking to him. John didn't try to fix me, he refrained from telling me what to do, and he withheld judgment. What he did do was listen and share some of his own experiences, which had proved to him that there is only one truth, one hope, and one answer to all the events of our fallen world. He told me his Father—the name he used for God—was also waiting to lift me in His arms and, with pure love, give me the assurance I needed. My friend told me God always had and always would see me as His child, and He would give me more than enough mercy, grace, and love to help me overcome and truly be free.

John then shared with me an incredible testimony of forgiveness—a testimony from his own life. It is not my story to share, but it's enough to say that my friend ventured into the high risk area of vulnerability, and the pain in his life and the level of forgiveness required of him equaled or surpassed my own. I appreciated John's story and his vulnerability. However, I could not appreciate the gift he was trying to give me. I did not believe I needed God's grace.

Instead, in a drunken rage, I called my mom and demanded she contact our old neighbor, who at one time provided transportation to and from St. Anne's for my sister and me. I recalled they were close to Father Chesterfield and would probably know if he was still alive and, if so, where he lived. My mom did make the call and told me Father Chesterfield was in fact alive. He was in an assisted living community only ten miles from my house.

Tomorrow! I made a silent and personal commitment to pay him a visit the next day. It was my intention not to overwhelm myself with some elaborate scheme. If I put too much thought into what I was going to do, I might not be able to follow through with it. Here I was, a drunk, divorced, absentee dad with a death wish, who wanted to confront a frail ninety-one-year-old respected priest who had dedicated his life to the church, celibacy, counseling married couples, and authoring numerous children's books. He was at an age in his life when he could no longer defend himself. Who was I to destroy the life of a godly man in his last days? What made the most sense to me was driving to an old folks home, first stopping for a twelve-pack of beer, drinking it in the parking lot, and then walking into the compound to simply say, "I have not forgotten what you did to me." That was it. After all the years, I wanted to tell him I hadn't forgotten, and it was exactly what I set out to do.

The next day, I drove to the community, drank the beer, walked in the main entrance, and approached the receptionist. "Can I help you, sir?" she politely asked.

"I would like to see Father Chesterfield, please," I answered.

The reality of what I was doing hit me when the woman knew exactly who I was talking about. I don't know why, but for some reason I thought I was going to have to explain who he was and who I was. The fact that she didn't need an explanation made Father Chesterfield real for the first time since the sexual abuse he committed against the boy I was three decades earlier on the church campus.

She has to know why I am here, I thought. I also wondered how many men before me made this same visit for the same reason.

The receptionist asked, "Is he expecting you?"

Of course he is, I thought. *He must have been expecting me for many years.* However, I simply said, "No."

"And what is your name?"

"I am Mike Rossman from St. Anne's church; he will know who I am."

I was a little concerned that she would smell the twelve beers I had chugged in the parking lot and call the police, but there was no indication she had. She suggested I take a seat while she went to see if he was feeling up to having visitors.

The woman quickly returned, her demeanor slightly changed. "I'm sorry, sir. Father Chesterfield is unavailable."

"May I leave him a note?" I asked.

She nodded, providing me a pen and paper. I simply wrote, "I am Mike Rossman from St. Anne's, and I would like to talk to you. Please call me." And I left my number.

When I walked out, I headed straight to the nearest bar, ordered a whiskey, and waited for a call from Father Chesterfield that he would never make.

CHAPTER 22

◄◦►

Making Accusations

For weeks, I went on an alcohol binge and waited. As a child, I had wished he would not show up or would die, but now I wanted him to call and to live long enough for me to face him. But my caller ID didn't reveal a number indicating Father Chesterfield was attempting to contact me. Though I obsessively checked my voicemail, his verbal acknowledgement of my pursuit was nonexistent. Then one day I realized that although I sometimes still felt like a child, I wasn't, and I was no longer stuck waiting for him to do something or not. I contemplated my next move. I knew one thing. I was not going to stop until I faced him or one of us died. With Father Chesterfield battling time and me battling addiction, death was near for both of us.

Drunk, I contacted my friend, neighbor, and business attorney and shared a slurred version of my story and what I wanted to do, asking if he could help. Being a wise man, he declined, but he gave me the name of a prominent attorney who made it his mission to help those abused by priests by holding accountable the ones responsible and the institutions scrambling to protect their reputation through any means necessary. Mr. Lewis had already filed and litigated numerous suits against the church and alleged pedophile priests, including highly publicized cases in Boston. I made the call, feeling empowered and drunk at the same time.

I scheduled the appointment, expecting to shock the noted and relentless legal activist by describing the horrific details of my past. I shared everything, but he was not at all shocked. He seemed to have heard it all before. But I could tell he believed me. However, what happened next was not what I expected. With compassion, Mr. Lewis delivered an emphatic warning, advising me to seek some other way to find healing for myself. "If it is validation from the church, a confession from the priest, or the revelation of truth you are after, you are wasting your time," he told me, adding, "and not only would I be wasting your time, but the engagement with the large religious institution would take an incredible toll on you both physically and emotionally." Mr. Lewis went on to describe how my idea of justice would quickly be crushed by the reality of a long and drawn out process intended to prove that I was not to be believed, to prove that what I claimed was either imagined or a lie.

The church's high-powered defense attorneys would have the jury ask themselves why I hadn't told anyone when I was a child. They would ask how it was even possible my parents were unaware the abuse took place, why the visible signs of a childhood rape were not detected, and why I waited until the present to make these claims. Mr. Lewis reminded me that even though Father Chesterfield was a younger man back then, what the jury would see was a fragile old man near death who had dedicated his life to the church and serving God. By contrast, the jury would see me as a grown man and not the child I once was. Further, the defense attorneys would tell the jury that because of my alcohol abuse, I was not credible, and they would present evidence documenting the bad choices I had made in my life, suggesting that I was simply looking for someone to blame. Mr. Lewis ended by saying, "I recommend you move on if at all possible."

It was possible, but I was unwilling to receive the only way to the life I longed to live. The only way was with and through my Savior, Jesus. I told Mr. Lewis I wanted to move forward and file the lawsuit. "I assure you I understand the risk, and I accept the consequences," I said. *Besides, I have already experienced far worse consequences than what attorneys can inflict,* I thought. I didn't ask what the current market value of my pain and suffering was, nor did he offer to monetize it.

As I embarked on my determined and ill-advised battle against Father Chesterfield and the church, I also filed paperwork seeking full custody of my son, Cole, who was four at the time. My ex-wife and I held joint-custody, with her as the primary caregiver, but the arrangement was not working. Between his mom's efforts to make it difficult for me to have set visitation without interference and my cancellations, we were only preparing an unstable groundwork for our son to stand on as we passed down the compounded weight of generational pain. Together we destructively began eroding Cole's true inheritance. He had known his own value and expected to be loved and treasured by both of us together, but through his experiences, the seed of doubt entered his thoughts and worry began to take hold. Our conflict contained all the familiar arguments common to custody disputes, and we were successful in proving we were both failing as Cole's parents.

However, I could not stay sober, and as a result, much of the time I spent with Cole was while I was under the influence of alcohol. This included driving intoxicated with my son in the car, putting his life and the lives of others in danger. As part of the process through which the courts decide what is in the best interest of a child, the parents participate in couples and individual counseling sessions, and the child attends sessions with a children's counselor. I attended both individual and couples counseling appointments drunk, and I took Cole to his appointments after I had been drinking. Although no one ever discovered I was drinking alcohol throughout this process, I was. The legal wrangling went on for over a year, and in the end, the court determined my ex-wife would receive full custody of Cole. For our son, the process ended without an understanding of the loss of his mom and dad raising him together.

CHAPTER 23

─◄○►─

Despair and Hope

MY CONDITION WORSENED, MY desire to die intensified, and my only purpose in life was to face Father Chesterfield. From my broken perspective, the path I was on looked familiar, and on many levels, it was all I had ever known. I was running down the wrong and deeply rutted track, shackled by the same fear as the generations before me. I was trying my best to do something right, but deep down I knew I could not break the chains through my own determination and self-will. Everything in my life demanded I accept this as fact. I was close to giving up all hope.

The process of filing the lawsuit against Father Chesterfield and the church began. First, I had to prove I attended St. Anne's during the time I claimed the abuse occurred. I contacted my mom to see what she might have, and she provided a photo of me receiving my First Communion with Father Chesterfield, along with the actual certificate. The certificate included my name, the name of St. Anne's, and the date on the card, which was April 7, 1974. There was a signature line for the pastor, but it was unsigned. I assumed, since Father Chesterfield was in charge of the ceremony, he should have signed the card but neglected to.

I also requested records covering the four years of my time at St. Anne's, but the request came back stating no such documents or files for Mike Rossman existed. Included was an acknowledgment that

St. Anne's held a full set of records for my sister, Lori, but nothing on me. To me, it seemed a quiet confirmation of the words spoken over me as a child. I really was nothing, nonexistent, and now I was clearly lost. The words of Father Chesterfield rang loud in my memory as I made one last push to overcome.

When I received word that the evidence of my childhood attendance at St. Anne's had been lost, or more likely had been removed, I hit the bottle hard. Enraged, I recklessly drove to my mom's apartment and, in a drunken tirade, told her how much I hated her and wished she was dead.

Not long after this, in the spring of 2003, Dusty moved in with me. She was extremely concerned about my drinking and visible downfall. We lived in a beautiful 5,000 square-foot custom home overlooking a pond in a neighborhood of expensive houses. My dad and I had built most of them. I knew everyone in the suburban community, and they knew me as a young, honest, and ambitious professional who was in control of his life and knew his future.

Then, for no logical reason, I started a landscape and water feature project on the side yard of our house. We lived on a corner lot, which meant both the project and I were on full display. Daily, I would spend a few hours in the morning at my office in town and then return home to work on the yard, after stopping at the local market to pick up a case of beer and the liquor store for a pint of vodka. I labored nonstop throughout the day and into the night, drinking the entire time. Neighbors with whom I had established relationships while building their new homes could see me stumbling around my yard—sometimes sobbing, while I quietly told myself, "It's only pokido." I no longer cared.

After weeks of hard physical work and binge drinking, I was ready to connect the water pump to electricity. Being a man of caution, I shut off a breaker to an individual fuse. My plan was to cut into an existing wire under the house and hardwire the commercial grade pump. Through an access door, I entered the dark crawlspace, uncoiling wire as I stumbled and then ran headfirst into a series of wooden beams. Eventually, I located the new power source, confident I had eliminated the risk of shock, and spliced the thick wire. The last thing I remember was an arc and a jolt. I had entered the crawlspace in broad daylight. When I finally came to, it was dark outside. I had no idea how many hours or days had passed.

Lying next to me was my dog, Swagger. Her given name was Maggie, but she strolled with such a swag, her nickname was far more appropriate. She was a large Rottweiler/Lab mix whom I had rescued from the pound years before, and she was a devoted companion. I would take her to work with me every day, and she would sit on the passenger side in the cab of my truck with her leg on the armrest of the door and her head draped out the window. When Swagger and I eased our way up to stoplights, her eyes would connect with the driver's eyes in the car next to us, and she would evoke a smile and often laughter. Even in some of my darkest times, Swagger made me laugh.

When I finally regained consciousness, I felt like I was in a coffin. I laid on my back staring at the wood planks over my head. I could hear footsteps above and knew it was Dusty in her high heels, pacing the house and looking for me. According to all the signs, I was home. My truck was in the driveway, the garage door was open, tools were scattered all over the yard, dirt had been tracked into the house, and there was a sea of empty beer cans. Eventually, I dragged myself out from under the house.

"Hi, Dusty!" I greeted her. "I have been either passed out or unconscious, I'm not sure which, under the house." She had wholeheartedly believed that she was either going to get the phone call or find me dead herself.

My experience under the house carried little impact, but I could tell what my actions were doing to Dusty. I continued drinking over the next few months but avoided causing any worrisome events. I knew the odds were increasingly against me, and I would do something devastating. So I reached a point where I decided to try to stop drinking.

We had invited our families over for Thanksgiving, so I picked that Thursday as my first day sober. I figured that if I was going to be miserable around my family, I might as well kill two birds with one stone. Instead, I spent the entire time isolated in my bedroom suffering through depression and withdrawals. My parents and sister could not understand the condition I was in and only rolled their eyes in disgust and disbelief. The fact I had chosen alcohol over my son, business, and loving girlfriend was beyond their comprehension. Dusty's parents, on the other hand, remained silent. Through their unspoken connection to my dependence on alcohol and suffering, they both abstained from judgment.

Dusty knew my condition was life-threatening, not only to me but also to others, since I would drive under the influence. She contacted John to see if he was willing to help her arrange for me to enter a recovery program. Mr. Lewis was also aware of my drinking, and he informed me that if I chose to continue down a self-destructive path, he could no longer represent me. Based on my condition, he said I was making it easy for the church's defense counsel to establish my extreme lack of credibility.

I wondered, *How do the opposing attorneys expect me to be if I am claiming the abuse adversely affected my life? If my life was perfect, wouldn't they argue that the abuse didn't take place due to a lack of symptoms from past trauma?*

Mr. Lewis then provided me with the contact information for a reputable drug and alcohol treatment center.

Through the coordinated efforts of Dusty and John, a week before Christmas 2003, I entered treatment for a thirty-day intensive inpatient program. At that point, Dusty and I had been together a year, and she was already driving me for the second time to a drug and alcohol center. Yet she did it with unconditional love and support. She always told me how proud she was of me, even though I was a broken man and the best I could do was admit I needed help.

While I entered inpatient care, Dusty decided she was going to stop drinking, and she was able to quit on her own. Unlike Dusty,

I couldn't stop on my own, and I knew it. That's why I didn't even pretend to resist going into rehab, where I could at least open myself to an offering of hope. I was not afraid, but I was torn. I wanted help, I wanted healing, and I wanted to be sober, but I knew it would take a miracle. I thought I knew what a miracle was, and based on my understanding, a supernatural event could not go back in time and reach the little boy who needed it. The boy was lost and forgotten. Now as a man, equipped with a lie, my eligibility to be set free was denied. I remained in the depths of darkness beyond the healing touch of restoration power. Believing this, my life's purpose was to prove my credibility in order to establish a worldly and worthless truth.

I preferred the walls of an institution that housed the spiritually sick. It provided an environment of safety, and I trusted the people who worked there. Most of the employees had battled addiction at some point in their lives. They had discovered that focusing on helping others provided them with purpose and helped them remain sober. I also felt an immediate connection to the other patients, who were grandparents, moms, dads, husbands, wives, sons, daughters, doctors, mechanics, lawyers, construction workers, educators, and so forth. In one way or another, we all arrived on our knees, on equal footing, which was not necessarily above sea level, and we were no longer able to manage our own lives.

I thrived within the structure that was provided and was a model patient. I found comfort in knowing that I did not need a diagnosis of cancer, a gunshot wound, or liver failure for the staff to know I was dealing with a life-threatening affliction and a deep wound crying out for healing. Not drinking was easy for me within the walls of a safe place.

Dusty and I talked on the phone at least once a day during scheduled breaks, and she attended all visiting hours held on Sundays. She was the only one who called and the only one who visited. I am grateful she did. On one of her Sunday visits, Dusty brought the tools of her trade to give me a haircut. We placed a chair out in the central courtyard, and I made my request: "Shave it all off." Without hesitation, she buzzed it all off. In typical fashion and on full display, we laughed. To this day, my haircut hasn't changed.

One Sunday, Dusty told me she had started attending church on Sundays with John and his wife. After the morning service, she would drive two hours to spend the afternoon with me. She described how much she enjoyed the pastor's message. In her uniquely enthusiastic way, complete with animated hand gestures, Dusty said, "I am certain the pastor was speaking directly to me." There was no denying her spiritual experience, and I was happy for her.

At the end of my thirty days, we celebrated the incredible transformation of those who completed the program and the hope that had been restored. Hope was not only present in those who grasped the idea of living one day at a time, but it could also be seen, albeit with reservation, in the family and friends who waited to take their loved ones home. I made friends with unlikely candidates, and we promised each other to stay out of trouble and keep in touch. I truly wanted to hold on to what I had learned and what I had gained. However, although I wanted to abstain from picking up the first drink, deep down I knew that in order to resume my determined course in confronting Father Chesterfield, I would drink again. Alcohol was the only thing making sense of my sickness and normalizing my irrational behavior.

CHAPTER 24

◄○►

My New Life

WITH THE EXCEPTION OF getting married in a church to my ex-wife, where I did sneak a few shots of Jack Daniels in the dressing room prior to the ceremony, I had not entered a church since I was eight years old. But after leaving rehab, I began attending Sunday service with Dusty. At first, I was nervous and battling a mild case of nausea, but it didn't take long for me to develop a level of trust and genuine appreciation for Pastor Ken, who I could tell was a kind and honest man. Pastor Ken gave me an opportunity to consider that what he preached from the Bible might actually be true. There was no doubt in my mind that he believed it was true, and as far as I could tell, he lived it.

After we attended my first Sunday service, Dusty and I stayed to visit with John and his wife. During the course of our conversation, John asked me if I would like to accept Jesus into my life as my Lord and Savior. Without hesitation, I accepted; I knew I needed a savior. John led me in prayer, and after we finished, he told me I was a new man and had been forgiven for all my sins—past, present, and future. It was good news. I had experienced plenty of sin in my past, and there was a good chance that there was more to come. The seed John had planted, over eighteen years before, finally penetrated my heart, and I was able to receive the gift of a new life. I was born again.

John told me God's love for me ran deep, and He had sent His only son to die on the cross for me so I could be saved and have eternal life in heaven. I listened, but an underlying question remained, keeping a shadow of doubt over my new life and the Father's love for me. *If He loves me so much,* I wondered, *why did He let those horrible things happen to me because of choices made by other men?* It was a good question. Eventually, I needed to follow it up with another question: *Why was I free to make countless bad choices myself?* Although I thankfully hadn't injured or killed anyone, I chose countless times to put others at risk by driving drunk. How different were my intemperate choices when held against those made by my grandfather and Father Chesterfield?

There were differences, but there were also many unknowns. I certainly didn't understand it then, and I do not fully understand it now. I expect I will not know the answer to this (and many more questions) until I get to heaven. However, what I have come to understand since my early days of accepting Jesus as my savior is that when I am grounded in truth and when truth is love, then peace is abundantly available. The reality of the gift of grace and the price paid for my forgiveness is it transcends all questions I may think I need answers to. This is the understanding I've come to now. At that time, I had no grid for how to process my question. I started on another journey, one taking me to the freedom I longed for.

But it didn't happen overnight. When I asked Jesus to be my savior, I didn't have a spiritual encounter or feel any different. For me, it would take more time to experience the renewing of my mind and the willingness to trust. But somehow, I knew God was not in a hurry. All I needed was to be aware of His love, patience, and kindness. In His eyes and from His enduring presence, He carried me through the pain and lifted me high above the pit. God loved me exactly where I was, and His plan did not involve me remaining there.

Although I didn't feel it at the time, a tiny part of me, maybe the boy I once was, who knew the value of what he had been given, grabbed hold of the promise and would not let go of the savior he longed for. The child inside me knew better than the man I had become, and little Mike embraced the promise that I was clean and made new in His perfect image. The forgotten boy understood my infinite value to our Father.

Dusty, being the wise woman she was, was not willing to let another minute go by in her life without Jesus. She accepted the Lord into her life on the same day and has not looked back. Truly, she is an incredible woman and proof that my Father loves me.

Following the day marking the true beginning of my transformation, I began meeting with John once a week for Bible study, which also included lengthy open and honest conversations. Relative to where I had been sixty days prior, I was doing well. This was a good thing. My heavenly Father doesn't waste time, and He began to pour blessings over my life. The year 2004 would bring my proposal and marriage to Dusty; the miracle of Dusty's pregnancy; the healthy birth of our daughter, Sophia; my increased ability to be a dad to Cole and the gift of quality time spent with him; and the groundbreaking for my most ambitious version of Sesame Street—a fourteen million dollar project.

Second Phase of Sesame St. Built in 2006

Through it all, I didn't pick up one drink the entire year, which truly was a miracle. However, even with alcohol removed, a void remained in my life due to my unwillingness to release control of the filling and measure of my renewed nature. Jesus could have everything else, but this one was mine.

It would have been a good time for me to embrace the fulfillment of all I wanted and all I would ever need in Jesus. It would have been the perfect time to stop looking back and drop my pursuit of my own justice in confronting Father Chesterfield. But I did not even consider it.

After a short engagement period, which started when I tied the ring to Swagger's collar and encouraged her to jump on the couch to deliver it, Dusty and I drove to California to get married. We stopped in the city of Redding to pick up our marriage license and continued on to the beautiful California coast. Our destination was a little resort beyond the Redwoods. I made friends with a gentleman during my time in treatment who owned and operated a picturesque inn situated high on a cliff above the Pacific Ocean. He graciously extended an open invitation for Dusty and me to come down and stay for a few days. I decided to take him up on the offer and figured it would be a perfect time and place for us to get married. It was a happy and peaceful time for us. I deeply loved my new bride.

Truly, it was a year of miracles for us. Thus, when December 2004 arrived, Pastor Ken asked Dusty and me if we would stand before the church body during the Christmas services to share our one-year testimony of giving our lives to Christ. I was sober, Dusty was about to give birth to our daughter, and we enthusiastically accepted his invitation—although I did have reservations.

I had previously shared my story with Pastor Ken, yet he was a conservative man and the leader of a conservative church, and he felt nervous about some of the content of my story. He asked us to testify about what God had done in our lives over the previous twelve months, and I could see the conflict in Pastor Ken's face when we met to review our stories. He didn't think it was appropriate for us to describe the abuse as being "sexual abuse" or to disclose the abuse as having occurred in a church and by a priest.

Part of me understood, particularly since children would be listening. I didn't question his decision. To be sure, a Christmas service would not have been the proper venue, but I couldn't help but wonder what would have happened if "proper" had been set aside many years ago, when Dusty and I were children, and we had heard a story exposing the secrecy of abuse that we believed we were living alone. Would it have inspired us to tell someone then? I do not know.

A few weeks later, Dusty and I stood on the stage and together shared the testimony of our miraculous year. Today, I still wonder whether it was the right decision. Certainly, the miracles God performed in our lives during the year after receiving Jesus were incredible all by themselves. Yet I can't help feeling something was lost when we left out the reality of where we came from and what we went through. What if I was granted freedom to be transparent about our past and, therefore, about our present struggles, too? Personally, I think it's good to let others know when our houses still need cleaning, to be truthful about human nature and our fears. As we share ourselves truthfully in a safe community, we learn to more fully trust our Father and can begin to let go of the things we're afraid to lose. One of my greatest challenges was letting go of the lies. The power in witnessing the raw vulnerability of someone in the midst of walking it out can profoundly communicate the truth that none of us are alone when we begin to release our grips.

Unfortunately, I had not yet been able to let go. Thus, a stark contrast existed in my life. On one hand, I was on my new walk with Jesus and had my testimony of God's love for me; on the other, I continued to pursue the litigation process and provided testimony of another man's sin. Also, I still hated myself. Both light and darkness existed in me.

Then, a few days after Christmas, on December 29, 2004, our beautiful daughter, Sophia Michelle Rossman, was born. Dusty has type 1 diabetes, and with it comes increased risk for both the mother and baby. The added complications are present throughout the pregnancy and increase during delivery. Watching Dusty care for our child in her womb by intentionally managing her disease with unwavering purpose for the well-being of our daughter caused a deeper love for her to spring up within me. Finally, after nine months, our healthy Sophia was born. To me, it was not only a sign of God's blessing but also of his forgiveness of me for my decision to abort our child years earlier.

God had already forgiven; Dusty and I still needed to.

CHAPTER 25

―◄〇►―

The Deposition

OVER THE NEXT THREE years, God continued to work in measurable ways in our lives. Best of all, He knew all the desires of our hearts, and He did not forget our wounds. Thus, His plan for us ran much deeper than we realized. Before we could begin receiving our true inheritance, we needed to begin walking (sometimes falling and then crawling) through the process of surrendering to His goodness. As children, our Father lovingly allowed us to hold on to whatever we needed to survive in a fallen world. It didn't matter whether it was the comfort of a smelly dog, some decomposing soccer socks, a cozy blanket, the fantasy of a savior (represented by a dad, mom, or big brother), a car, or even a massive tree; they were ours to keep and to hold. But now our Father wanted much more for Dusty and me. He wanted us to know the truth, to experience authentic freedom, and to thrive through the life of His Son Jesus. Most of all, He wanted us to let go of the lies we had believed for so long, to be grounded in truth, and to begin building our new lives on the foundation of His love.

This, of course, was not clear to us at the time. The process was often painful and terrifying. But with Jesus by our sides, always there to pick us back up, we took baby steps along the path toward the arms of our Father.

In mid-February 2005, after a year of experiencing levels of peace beyond what I found on my own efforts and freedom from addiction, I sat in a downtown Portland high- rise building waiting for depositions to begin, led by the attorneys representing Father Chesterfield and the church. In the previous twelve months leading up to the deposition, I had had little contact with Mr. Lewis and had received limited information specific to my case. While guardedly waiting for a gesture to signal it was my turn to enter the private room, Mr. Lewis did his best to prepare me for what to expect. He explained the questioning would not be as pressing and strategic as what I would face in trial, but nonetheless, it would be difficult.

I was in the law offices of one of the largest and most prominent firms in the state, and I felt small. A woman named Mrs. Donovan was lead counsel for Father Chesterfield and the church, and when questioning began, I immediately found myself wanting to like her. I wondered how she could separate her professional career from her personal life. Mrs. Donovan was obligated, of course, to be calculating in her defense. I also wondered if hearing these testimonies caused Mrs. Donovan, as a mom, to protect and love her kids a little more. Or was it possible that formal education and the drudgery of the justice system had allowed her to block out the stories of those claiming sexual abuse at the hands of her clients. To be sure, some of her clients were innocent men who were telling the truth. But others were guilty, protecting themselves at the cost of a child's innocence.

When the examination began, the initial questions were for my legal name, social security number, address, and other questions to prove I was in fact the same person as the child left in the care of the church decades earlier. Although I wanted to like the opposing attorney, I didn't expect to, yet out of nowhere, Mrs. Donovan said she noticed I was quite the soccer player, giving an indication that she had reviewed my files thoroughly. Mrs. Donovan exuded experience, professionalism, and a hardened shell, yet for some reason, she also let me know she was a mom. "My daughter plays the same position on her soccer team," she said.

Abruptly, the small talk ended, the atmosphere shifted, and the questioning began in earnest. The following are portions of the certified transcripts representing the sensitive, humiliating, and painful examination of my past by Mrs. Donovan (more graphic questions were intentionally left out). It lasted more than three hours. How sad it was to be a man depending on a little boy's memory to answer sexually charged questions. God did not create the mind of a child to recall the details of such terrifying events.

> Q: Was there a pattern to the way it would happen, the place where it would occur, the times it would happen?
>
> A: The only thing I remember is wanting to be invisible and him walking in to the room and calling on me, so specific patterns, I don't.
>
> Q: Do you know how many times there was inappropriate contact between you and Father Chesterfield in this room in the church building?
>
> A: No.
>
> Q: And when you were in the second grade, between the fall of '72 and the spring of '73, did the rapes take place in the same places that you previously described.
>
> A: Yes.
>
> Q: What is your best estimate as to the number of times that you engaged in sexual contact with Father Chesterfield in your third grade year between the fall of '73 and the spring of '74?
>
> A: It would remain consistent with the first two years, first grade and second grade.

[I wondered, *When did it become possible for a six-year-old child to engage in sexual contact with a man? I didn't recall having a choice.*]

Q: Did anyone ever catch you having sexual contact with
     Father Chesterfield?
A: No.

[Again I wondered, *As a child, how could it have been me who
instigated the contact? Why was I the one who needed to be caught?*]

Q: Did you ever tell anyone about the sexual contact
     between you and Father Chesterfield?
A: No.
Q: Why did you stop going to the church after your First
     Communion?
A: I never wanted to go back again.
Q: And why is that?
A: Because of what took place while I was there.
Q: When he would come to pick you up at your home and
     take you to CCD, would he come in the house?
A: No.
Q: What kind of car did he drive?
A: A black station wagon.
Q: Did Father Chesterfield have any distinguishing
     features that come to mind?
A: Big hands.
Q: What is Springbrook?
A: It's a drug and alcohol treatment center.
Q: Okay. And you were there for alcohol treatment?
A: Yes.
Q: And it's probably self-evident, but you were there
     because you were struggling with issues related to
     alcohol?
A: Yes.
Q: You've written, "Because of my childhood experiences,
     I made a promise to myself that I would ensure that
     my son had a safe, secure, and happy childhood."

A: Yes.

Q: When did you make that promise to yourself?

A: When I first discovered my ex-wife was pregnant with Cole.

Q: Part of the promise that you made to yourself when you realized that you were going to have a child was that you were going to create an environment so that your son would not be sexually abused. Is that a fair statement?

A: Yes.

Q: Do you recall your father considering you a little crybaby?

A: Yes.

Q: Was that difficult for you?

A: Yes.

Q: You say, "He always wished I was more like him." Is that the feeling you had when you were growing up?

A: Yes.

Q: Were you like your father?

A: No.

Q: How were you two different?

A: Well, my view of my father was he was the strong— physically strong person that really didn't fear anything whereas I seemed to fear everything.

Q: Did your father ever ask you when you were crying, what the problems were?

A: Not that I remember.

Q: Okay. You've certainly had your struggles with alcohol?

A: Yes.

Q: Has anyone ever accused you of sexually abusing Cole?

A: No.

After three hours, when Mrs. Donovan was done, she told me we would need to schedule more depositions.

It was awful. Although I didn't have a drink in my hand, I had already relapsed. It was a matter of time until my relapse manifested. Unfortunately, it happened in the context of my insecurities about parenting.

CHAPTER 26

—◀◉▶—

Back to the Bar Stool

DUSTY AND I WERE determined to raise our child differently, and one of our long-term priorities was to ensure Sophia always had her mommy or daddy home with her while the other was at work. Dusty remained on maternity leave for three months after Sophia was born, and her motherly bond was permanently sealed. Yet she could not stay home forever. Dusty did her best to adjust emotionally in preparation for the day she would return to work, but work was far from where her heart was. Above all else, her dream was to be a mom and a loving wife and to receive unconditional love. With the gift of Cole as her stepson (whom she loved), the arrival of Sophia, and the reality of a sober husband to love and who loved her, Dusty's life was as she always dreamed it would be.

Prior to meeting me, Dusty had also been married. To family, friends, and acquaintances, they presented a fun and outgoing couple. By all appearances, they were genuinely happy, and there was much to look forward to in the years ahead. However, Dusty entered marriage with the expectation each could fill the void in the other—the void occupied by hurt, abandonment, and anger. Instead, she quickly found a reflection of all she had ever known, the recognition of pain. Entirely unaware of the hidden source of pain and the depths of suffering the other experienced prior to entering each other's lives, they both zeroed in on the other's inability to find healing. They didn't know how to love, but they knew how to hurt. It wasn't long until their marriage ended.

However, after accepting Jesus, Dusty grew rapidly in her relationship with her Father. Although for a long time I didn't want to admit it, she progressed in her spiritual growth much faster than I did. As part of her spiritual awakening, Dusty flowed right into her gift as an amazing mom and the heavenly joy it brought her. This is what she wanted to do full-time. Fortunately, because we were both self-employed, we were partially able to make it possible for her to be a stay-at-home mom, with the exception of three days during the week. Dusty figured it was in everyone's best interest to keep her closest clients, whom she enjoyed visiting with, and to use the time talking to them.

At the same time, my business was growing. My partner (who from the beginning didn't have any idea he was partnering in building Sesame Street, let alone who he was partnering with) and I had completed our first development project a few years earlier, and the impressive building had three stories of apartments above retail space. Dusty operated her business in one of the storefronts.

Based on the plan Dusty and I had put together, I would be solely responsible for our daughter three days a week (which included Sophia going to the office with me), in addition to spending time with Cole. I was terrified. I continued to battle the belief that my only contribution to raising our daughter and my son was through financial security. I was under the illusion that money, nice clothes, and family status—representing success—provided a layer of protection. I thought it would somehow keep a target off my kids and scare away those looking for vulnerability through neglect. The approach also allowed me to love my entire family from a distance. By maintaining an intentional disconnect, I honestly believed I was doing them all a favor.

Eventually, my first day as a stay-at-home dad arrived. *What do I do now?* I thought with anxiety. I still couldn't decipher a situation of safety from one of danger, and I defaulted to the only one proven real in my life. My daughter's innocence was precious and valuable, and I trembled at the thought of her innocence being taken. *I am not capable of protecting it,* I thought, agreeing with the lie. The recent deposition had left me spinning with raw emotion and had allowed past lies to regain a foothold. Once again, these lies began to overtake the truth I had started to trust. All I knew from my past was that the unimaginable was possible. My grandfather and Father Chesterfield confirmed the reality that bad things happen. I was not concerned about my own safety or worried I would become the direct cause of harm to my daughter. The problem was, I had no context to believe I could protect her.

By this time in my life, I could clearly remember the little boy I once was, and because I had not been able to protect him, I believed I could not protect my own kids either. Knowing the devastation, fear, and pain caused by my own childhood trauma, I knew I would not be able to live with myself if something happened on my watch. I didn't know how to conquer these lies because I didn't fully trust the Father and His truth. As a result, I continued to meditate on this fear and paralyzing anxiety about the possibility of my own children being subject to a life filled with affliction took over.

While Dusty worked in the salon—like my grandma did thirty-four years before, when my grandfather watched over my sister and me—I panicked and called my sister Lori and asked her to come to my house and be with Sophia. Then I drove straight to the bar, where I couldn't get the whiskey down fast enough. Like the five-year-old boy with the Hoppity Horse, I intentionally deflated the hopes of my wife and the family I had begun to love.

During the first year after accepting Jesus into my life, when I remained sober and began to experience God's peace, a hidden darkness remained deep within me. When I decided to return to the isolation of a bar stool, my peace quickly drowned and my anger ignited. My internal desire for vengeance became a driving force of self-destruction, and the litigation process and pain overtook the ground I had recently released to Jesus.

I did my best to reassure Dusty my intensions were not to return to a drunken stupor. I wanted to believe it, too, but secretly I knew

I intended to drink until the day I faced Father Chesterfield. Back then, the truth was vague; now it is vivid. When I surrendered my own will to God, peace and His presence allowed me to breathe, and with each new cleansing breath, I was made new. He took care of what I couldn't. But when I took back control, I stopped trusting my Father understood I wanted to stand before Father Chesterfield as a much stronger man and to pry his frigid hand from the back of my neck. But God did know, and He knew better than me. He knew *I* was the one who needed to release my grip on Father Chesterfield and my grandfather—to forgive them so I could run as a child to a loving place He had created for me.

Before long, alcohol once again became my primary focus, although I intentionally abstained from drinking daily, reserving it for times when I needed it to stay the course in my pursuit of the destruction of Father Chesterfield—which I masterfully disguised as justice. Occasionally, Dusty would be suspicious and ask if I had been drinking. Trying to hold back my defensiveness, I would adamantly deny it.

A few months passed in this way, and from Dusty's perspective, life for us was going well. We continued to attend church, and I still met regularly with John for continued guidance and Bible study and to talk about the blessings and challenges in our lives. The difference between Dusty and me during this time was that her eyes were centered on the Lord, while mine were on Father Chesterfield. Thus, her walk progressed while I did my part to remain anchored in resentment. I was not growing in my relationship with Jesus, yet despite my poor choices, I continued to experience a shift in how I struggled. My actions certainly created consequences, but my Father's plan did not alter. He continued to move me gently from a state of hopelessness, while stabilizing the ground I would eventually stand on. In the past, when I slipped, I felt the freefall into darkness, but now I experienced a constant and gentle tug pulling me toward the light of a new hope, even though I was still unable to trust it.

CHAPTER 27

◄◦►

Living on Sesame Street

Dusty and I decided it was time to simplify our lives. In 2005, we sold our big house, which stored an excessive amount of painful memories, along with most of our stuff. We held a giant two-day garage sale at which Dusty performed as a top sales associate. We both marveled at the joyful ease with which we unloaded items we originally purchased because we thought they would make us happy. I know for sure we experienced more fun getting rid of everything as partners than we did accumulating it alone.

All our stuff would not fit in our garage but had spilled out over the driveway, yard, and sidewalk. We had no choice but to have a garage, yard, and sidewalk sale, all in the same weekend; it all needed to go. Our new home, which was located in one of our apartment buildings, was smaller than our stately three-car garage. Our flat was three floors above the salon where Dusty worked, and my office was two blocks down the street. In the process of our move, God revealed He had never forgotten my dream. The special day arrived. *I remember the significance of my childhood dream, and I can't believe it is actually happening,* I thought to myself, pausing to reflect on the magnitude of what was taking place. My family and I were moving to Sesame Street.

During this whole process, I continued to drink occasionally and do my best to hide it from Dusty. Although riddled with anxiety, I was able to keep it together during my time with Sophia as well as maintaining my visitation schedule with Cole.

I was already two years into the legal process, and after my deposition, I received periodic calls from Mr. Lewis, asking me questions and providing updates. It wasn't unusual, however, for months to pass without me hearing a word, and I filled the gaps through reading media reports and articles, as there was an increasing amount of coverage during this time. Occasionally, I visited websites set up by groups of men who, as boys, had suffered in silence at the mercy of abusive priests. There I read familiar accounts of how survivors all over the world struggled to fit in and cope. Not many had testimonies of healing and finding peace. The dysfunction resulting from sexual abuse was consistent—shattered lives made worse through addiction, broken relationships, job loss, and incarceration. I was moved by the frequency of posts written by family members honoring a dad, son, or brother who had ended the affliction with suicide.

I understood the inherent risk in reading about a hurtful truth while my mind was vulnerable, but it was truth, and it was ugly. I identified with these broken men just as Jesus continues to identify with the sufferings of all of us. The mistake and danger for me was in processing the information and feelings through my old self—the part of me I held on to and refused to surrender. Non-Christians and Christians alike advised me to block out my past and move on, but I refused to listen.

Someone I met with often, and who did not believe in Jesus, pointed me to the famous Shakespeare quote—"To thine own self be true." The quote, mounted strategically, hung above her desk, where I would stare at it for long periods as we discussed business. I tried to grasp it with confidence and live it with pride, but the problem was that my own truth was a lie, and I didn't know it. My truth was my perspective, a perspective grounded in lies passed down for generations and reinforced by tolerance of ungodly things, which ultimately led to a compromise in morality. Combined, tolerance and compromise open the door to the undermining of truth and the erosion of hope.

Because of these things, my frustration increased when other Christians counseled me to forget the past and move on. Though I doubt they intended it this way, their advice communicated that God was not big enough to redeem the sinner who had committed the sexual abuse and to restore to wholeness the one who was abused, while also providing forgiveness and restoration in all relationships destroyed on both sides. I needed a Father who could do *all* things. I now know my Father was not asking me to discard my past, ignore the pain, or conform to the teachings of this world. Rather, He wanted me to see all things through the eyes of Jesus, with a renewed mind, a changed heart, and hope grounded in truth. From His truth, all things are possible, and victory is already accomplished.

Fortunately for me, I was not capable of wearing my Father out. As hard as I tried (and I did try), I could not prove He didn't love me, and I couldn't push His patience and kindness to the breaking point. Never did He tell me or show me He could not help; never did He leave me and move on to those souls easier to save or wounds easier to heal.

Some of the people in my life who loved me went to great lengths to help. They took incredible risks and sacrificed time, and because of their genuine—yet ineffective—efforts to help me, they ended up disappointed and hurt. I wanted help, but I could not trust it or receive the emotional support people offered. As a result, many of the relationships did not end well. It seemed like the more these good-hearted, well-intentioned people tried, the worse things got for all involved, and with good reason, they moved on.

In the fall of 2005, Dusty and I became official members in our church, and I volunteered for janitorial services, attended a morning Bible study, and participated in a faith-based recovery program. Dusty enjoyed the fellowship with other moms she found by volunteering in the nursery and Sunday school. And when our church sent a mission team to New Orleans to help after Hurricane

Katrina, Dusty decided to go along. It was a significant decision for her, representing her growing walk with the Lord. It was also her first extended time away from Sophia.

As she continued to grow in her faith, I continued to struggle. How was it, after being saved, that I still secretly believed I was an absolute failure as a dad? I was convinced I was nothing and would always be nothing. Yet, as convinced as I was, persuading God to come into agreement with a lie is not possible. My problem was what I believed about myself—beliefs forced upon me by my abusers and subtly reinforced by my own family, who felt the same about themselves. Because I was not yet willing to forgive those who had hurt me, I could not get free of the lies they'd told me about myself. Of course, God knew what I believed about myself was a lie. By the grace of God, my ignorance and inability to know I was blessed was powerless to alter His perfect plan for my life.

In early 2006, Dusty and I received the miraculous news that she was pregnant, and not only was she pregnant, she was carrying twins. I believed I was already failing two beautiful children, and now it was going to be four, but when I heard the news, my response was excitement and joy. Dusty's joy was more reserved; she was concerned about how I would handle it. Three months into Dusty's pregnancy with twins, at our scheduled ultrasound, the doctor entered the room to let us know that one of the babies had not survived. But the doctor assured us that the other was healthy and doing well. The news was hard for both of us, and I tried to process and make sense out of what was going on inside me. *Why is this so difficult for me?* I wondered. *Why am I feeling such sadness over the loss of a child I did not know?* With those feelings came the revelation that life made more sense to me than death. I was grateful our other child was alive and thriving. Cole and Sophia's little brother, Luke William Rossman, was born on October 16, 2006.

All in all, it was another year of meaningful favor for me and my family. Dusty, once again, remained strong throughout her pregnancy and delivery, resisting the complications of diabetes and contending for her health and the health of Luke. And I continued my slow and gradual improvement as a dad and husband, while we celebrated the completion of our largest development project to date, along with the simultaneous groundbreaking of a new one. Dusty and I planned to move our growing family into one of the loft units we had specifically designed for ourselves; our new home was going to be located in Phase III of Sesame Street.

Final Phase of Sesame St. Built in 2008

CHAPTER 28

―◦―

The Station Wagon

ACTIVITY SURROUNDING MY LAWSUIT picked up during the summer of 2006, and the attorneys for Father Chesterfield and the church deposed my dad, mom, and Dusty. Mr. Lewis' office conducted telephone interviews with my sister, John, and business associates, along with parents from my old neighborhood who, decades earlier, had provided transportation to St. Anne's for my sister, their own children, and me. As a man, I felt ashamed and embarrassed people were called to answer questions about my past, however, as a child, I would have done anything for those calls to be made. Through the process of accepting the burden, shame, and humiliation and allowing the dissection of my life on behalf of a forgotten child, I gained personal understanding. I was also willing to do anything for my own children.

Due to the large volume of claims against individual priests and the church, I became part of a class action lawsuit and was required to participate in mediation. With many claims filed, and many more pending, church officials were concerned about the amount of money spent on attorney fees for its defense. Judges were also concerned about the potential strain placed on public resources and the court system, even if only a fraction of the cases went to trial. The financial implications became so great, the church filed for bankruptcy protection. All stakeholders on the side of the defense, along with the neutral parties, such as the courts, hoped mediation would allow a cost-effective way to resolve the mounting lawsuits, which set in motion far-reaching financial implications.

Prior to mediation, Dusty and I arrived at the same law offices where the depositions took place, and we met Mr. Lewis in a coffee shop located in the lobby. He wanted to spend a few minutes with us explaining how negotiations would proceed during the mediation process. Mr. Lewis made it clear, even though I was required to participate in mediation, I was not required to agree to any terms in settling my case.

"This is going to be a difficult day," Mr. Lewis said, adding, "I am concerned for both of your well-being." He told us I was about to face the challenges he warned me about at the beginning of the process.

Mr. Lewis had more to say, but Dusty interrupted him, and in a caring voice, she said, "This must be hard for you."

Mr. Lewis paused, losing his train of thought, and then began to cry, warning me, "Father Chesterfield is in the building."

It was the first and only time I would see the emotional toll the process placed on Mr. Lewis. I understood. For many of these men who were his clients, he was the hope and voice for the broken, looking for answers. His clients fully depended on him to help and strengthen them as they made one final push to overcome the affliction, one last attempt to be free. I admired the courage and work Mr. Lewis did for both the forgotten children and the men they became, but I did not envy his position. His work was only part of a process; in itself, legal action is ineffective at providing the miracle of healing or delivering on the promise of freedom.

Within the same law offices, but in separate rooms, Father Chesterfield would be with his attorneys, and down the hall, Dusty and I would be with Mr. Lewis. Information from both sides was going back and forth in an attempt to find common ground and settle the case. I felt a sense of empowerment knowing Father Chesterfield was required to attend the meeting, but at the same time, I was nervous that he was near. Father Chesterfield probably had long forgotten the damaging words he had spoken over me, but I had not. As a man, I sat in the room feeling uncertain of what might happen and shamefully afraid because he knew I had told what he did to me.

I felt like I had done something terribly wrong. It was a familiar fear, similar to a frightened child. I was not only waiting to see what Father Chesterfield and his attorneys were going to do; I waited to see what the Devil was going to do. After all, he had been waiting patiently for me to open my mouth all these years. Yet even in the midst of my fear and vulnerability, I also wanted to see what my Father, who was always watching, was going to do.

What is God going to do? With that question, in that moment, I proved beyond a reasonable doubt that I was on the slow track for the faithfully challenged in learning awareness and developing trust. Was it not my deepest desire to be free through having the courage to confront my past? Hadn't I embarked on a journey a few years before to seek out and find truth, claiming victory through Jesus over the demons holding me in bondage? Since I was a boy, had I not wanted to tell my story and have it assuredly heard? While in despair, did I not pray for the strength to interrupt, disrupt, shake up, and shatter not only a generational curse within my family but also within an institution? Had I not asked God to give me wisdom to put an end to the far-reaching and devastating effects? I think so. And who was orchestrating all of this? God, of course. He was the facilitator of *all* the events working together for good, while Jack Daniels was scrambling to maintain a stronghold.

Mr. Lewis, Dusty, and I sat in a small conference room with glass walls overlooking the corridor. While the three of us were nervously engaging in small talk, Mr. Lewis said, "There he is."

Walking by the windows was a small, frail, hunchbacked old man. It didn't matter what he looked like; it didn't matter how much time had passed. Knowing it was the same man who had ruthlessly swept away my innocence when I was a boy paralyzed me, even though I was now a man and could have easily overpowered him. I felt his presence, and immediately, according to Dusty and Mr. Lewis, I turned white, and my shirt became soaked in sweat.

"I do not want to postpone," I answered, when given the opportunity. "I want to continue."

It seemed like hours passed before someone knocked on the door and asked Mr. Lewis to step out of the room. When he returned, he said, "Father Chesterfield's attorneys are having difficulty with some of your timelines and details from your deposition."

Mr. Lewis said Father Chesterfield's council challenged him on the difficult task of proving my case if it went to trial. As he relayed this information to us, he also told us their tactic was a typical defense strategy. Periodically, over the span of a few hours, Mr. Lewis stepped out of the room for further discussions. Each time he returned, he asked me to confirm statements or provide certain details previously provided in my deposition, which I did to the best of my ability.

Finally, after several hours of silence and suspense, broken only occasionally for brief answers to questions, Mr. Lewis returned to tell us the defense found my credibility lacking due to my alcohol abuse. Further, the attorneys fixed on one particular detail in my deposition, which caused them to place my overall account of what had happened in serious doubt. The attorneys acknowledged something may have happened, but likely not in the way that I remembered it.

I am sure there were other discrepancies in the exact details after thirty years, but the one detail Father Chesterfield's and the church's attorneys focused on was the color of Father Chesterfield's station wagon. I said it was black. They argued Father Chesterfield's station wagon was white, not black.

Mr. Lewis was correct all along, I privately acknowledged. In its entirety, specific to the lawsuit, litigation is unavailing in finding truth, even though I mistakenly believed it had to be. I wanted confirmation my Father was watching over me, and I wanted a sign

Jesus was sitting next to me in the room. But God did not do what I expected Him to do.

Disappointed, I decided to walk away. When I walked out of the law offices and entered the elevator, it was a slow and hopeless decent. I reengaged my independence and determined once I walked out the large glass doors alone, reentering a world I was helpless and unfit to change, I was taking back control of my life.

CHAPTER 29

—◆◇▶—

On My Terms

ONLY DAYS LATER, I began drinking again—drinking heavily. This time, I did not attempt to hide it from Dusty or anyone else.

One of the demands that Mr. Lewis was negotiating with the defense attorneys on my behalf was for me to have a controlled confrontation face-to-face with Father Chesterfield. During such a meeting, someone would accompany Father Chesterfield, and someone else would be present to ensure the intense encounter did not escalate into a harmful or threatening situation. Up until mediation, no financial terms were discussed nor any offers made by the attorneys representing Father Chesterfield and the church; the confrontation was the only thing I specifically asked for. I wanted a confession. I wanted the truth told, and I believed I deserved an apology. But by this time, it was clear I was not going to receive any of those things.

Believing it would discredit me as a man and minimize the trauma I experienced during my childhood, I did not verbalize my thoughts regarding what a large financial settlement would mean to me. I did, however, secretly consider what I would do if awarded millions of dollars by a jury or was paid the same to sign a confidentiality agreement. I thought about paying off my debts and securing my family's financial future while eliminating my responsibility to answer to anyone, including God. It would give me a false freedom, enabling me to kill myself on my own terms.

Father Chesterfield did not agree to my request, and his attorneys supported and defended the position based on his age and poor health. His defense believed that sitting across a table from me would overwhelm him, causing unnecessary stress to his ailing body. If I had been in their shoes, I would have taken the same position. Apparently, God did too, even though it was my most requested demand. I felt God owed me this one, but He did not deliver.

Mr. Lewis is an excellent attorney, and he fought diligently for me on this issue. But God, my Father, knew the long-term consequences and resulting burden such a meeting would have for my conscience and me. If I was allowed to face Father Chesterfield directly, in an attempt to force him to shamefully confess his secrets, subjecting a frail, tired, and already suffering old man to tremendous stress, it would have gained me nothing. Instead, God lovingly removed the responsibility from me, promising me He would avenge and repay on my behalf. My Father had me on a direct path to freedom. His plan for me was to overcome evil with good.

However, in my mind, this decision was an injustice. After all, Father Chesterfield did not consider my age and my condition when he made the decision to abuse me. The defense's refusal to settle on my terms by allowing the confrontation began to play a significant part in my daily routine. I intentionally began to stir up resentment, anger, and hatred in my heart. I believed I needed to tell Father Chesterfield that if he ever touched me again, I would kill him—like my dad had done to end the abuse from his father. To be a man, I required of myself an abusive resolution to an abusive past.

Each morning, without exception, I drove to a dark, seedy bar, sometimes waiting in the parking lot for the neon sign to read OPEN. There I drank at least two beers before opening the newspaper to check the obituaries. If Father Chesterfield was as close to death as his attorneys claimed, I thought his name should appear in print any day.

When his name did not appear, I felt betrayed, manipulated, and lied to and spent the remainder of the day drinking beer and whiskey. Yet I also knew if his name did appear, I would become angry, feeling robbed of my right to face the man who had caused me so much pain. Resentments would justify my ongoing self-destruction through alcohol. I knew, too, that even if they honored me by granting me the opportunity to face Father Chesterfield and hear a full confession and a heartfelt apology from him and the church, I would still be the same angry and bitter drunk. No matter what happened, I was going to spend my days in bondage. This was my plan. I picked up my addiction exactly where I had left it a few years before, at my lowest point, and I set forth to take it to new depths.

Surprisingly, I managed to hold on to some residue of dignity, and I would change my drinking venue so it wasn't obvious my entire day was spent on a barstool. More importantly, I did not want to get cut off by the bartender. One day, while I was in the process of changing locations, I stopped at a market a few blocks from my office to buy a can of chewing tobacco. As I sat in my truck, opening the can, Dusty and the kids pulled up next to me. Dusty immediately knew I had been drinking, but my kids, unable to understand my condition, were excited to see me. Dusty, whose hope had been growing and was then crushed, was now in protection mode for our children, and she drove off upset and angry.

Later, she explained to me, when she drove away, she looked in her rearview mirror and saw our two little kids sitting in their car seats and reflected on what it would be like if a drunk driver were to hit them, killing our two children. Dusty also asked herself, *What if Mike ends up being the drunk who kills an innocent family?* She made the correct decision and called 911.

After I saw Dusty and the kids, my conscience started bothering me, pressuring me to surrender and turn back to God. Instead of going directly to another bar, I decided to go to my office and work for a few hours. When I pulled out of the store's parking lot, traveling less than a block, I noticed two police cars. It was always momentarily sobering when I saw the police because I did not want to get caught drinking and driving. Apparently, I believed my actions were acceptable as long as I didn't get caught, get in an accident, or injure or kill someone. When I turned onto the street where my office was located, four police cars followed me with their lights flashing and sirens blaring. They pulled me over in front of my office, where I was visible to those working in my own business as well as many others on the street and in the surrounding area who knew me—people who thought they knew me as a family man, a successful real estate developer, and a man of integrity.

I walked with one foot in front of the other, up and down the sidewalk, forgetting the rest of my instructions while I focused on not stumbling. Cars slowly passed by, the passengers trying to get a closer look to see if they recognized the careless drunk. People gathered at their windows and porches to watch. Whether all these people knew me or not, what they saw was a representation of who I was. I did not want to be a drunk, and I did not want to hurt or kill anyone because of my drinking, but I also did not want to live in pain, at least not behind the illusion of a man who appeared to have everything.

As I stood in front of the officer, trying to connect my finger with the tip of my nose, the rapid pace of the world slowed. I was not nervous about the trouble I was in; I didn't care. I knew I was going to be less afraid locked up in a small holding cell than wandering aimlessly in a world I could not control. I remained calm, not attempting to convince the officers I was fine, and I failed the test, thinking only about losing the freedom and choice to return to the bar after my arrest. Handcuffed, I remained on display, standing along the side of the police car while the tow truck arrived to haul my vehicle to impound. Eventually the officers transported me to the county jail, where they confirmed my blood alcohol level was over the legal limit to drive; it was only eleven o'clock in the morning.

It was not my first time riding in the back of a police car or doing something unlawful, but it was the first time I broke the law and experienced the consequences. This experience was different from the time when, as a twelve-year-old boy, I rode as a passenger in a sheriff's car while on an adventure with my dad. Yet compared to other childhood rides in a neighbor's car or Father Chesterfield's station wagon, this was an improvement. At least now I was guilty, and I knew why I was held captive and punished. I felt at ease on my way to jail, knowing why it was optional to remain silent while shackled. Actually, I did speak, telling the police officers the truth about how much I drank. Part of me found comfort and freedom in controlling the punishment I had received. At the same time, I could not escape the conviction I felt in the back seat of the police car. I knew I was making wrong choices, but I wanted to hold on to my freedom to choose, regardless of the consequences.

The circumstances and consequences I continued to face were a result of holding on to lies capable of reinforcing the physical, emotional, and spiritual abuse I experienced as a child. In finding my freedom to choose as a man, I made choices from a broken perspective.

Yet on that car ride, something significant happened inside me. It didn't look significant on the outside. It was a shift in my mind—the kind of shift only God could make possible. It wasn't even new information, but for the first time, I internalized it. Suddenly, I believed deep down inside me that changing how I looked on the outside did not change anything within me. A superficial makeover was not going to mask previous generations, my childhood, or my family, and it surely was not going to change me. Until I was truly transformed on the inside, I would not have a foundational truth empowering me to rise above circumstance, and I would not have absolute hope to pass on to my own children. Image is nothing unless it is the glorious image of God.

Time continued to slow, even pause, while I sat in jail overnight. I had always felt imprisoned anyway, and I wondered whether my life might be easier in a small cell. After all, there I wouldn't have to question whether my neighbors were manipulative, deceitful, or violent. I would know for sure. To me, the confinement felt safer than surrounding myself with people who seemed to be kind and honest but might be the opposite.

My confinement was brief. While I sat on the cold steel bench in my cell, I worried about my release. When I learned I was free to go the next morning, I walked out of jail and directly into a bar, trying to get alcohol into my system before I was forced to think about the previous twenty-four hours. After reconnecting with the familiarity of a bar stool and a few shots of whiskey, I called for a taxi to take me to retrieve my truck.

CHAPTER 30

—◄○►—

Trying to Die

WHEN I TURNED FROM God, I stopped attending church, believing it signified the ultimate rejection of my Savior. I believed I deserved punishment for my actions. I saw and believed in God through the same broken perspective I saw everything else. It is true. God was always watching, and He did not miss a single sinful thought or action, but He saw those as separate from who I was as His son. Jesus looked upon me with compassion and from the perspective of our Father's endless and unchanging love. Part of my ongoing transformation would someday include no longer seeing through my own eyes but through the eyes of Jesus. This would include the miracle of looking inward and loving what I saw.

But I was not there yet. Instead, I was engaged in a silent and passively aggressive protest against the church, which made little sense since I liked the church I attended. Dusty continued to attend Sunday service without me. She also maintained the relationships she had developed and valued. Seeking help and guidance, Dusty discussed my relapse with our pastor, expressing in detail her main concern to him, which was my determination to fulfill a death wish. Without judgment, but without understanding the depths of my struggle, Pastor Ken suggested we schedule a time for the three of us to meet regularly for counseling. He genuinely cared for Dusty and me, and his offer was out of love and not merely an obligation of his job.

I accepted his invitation and proceeded to waste our pastor's time. Our counseling appointments focused on the fact our marriage was falling apart. But I was not in denial. I knew my actions were destroying Dusty, our kids, and our marriage, and I did not need someone to point out I was doing the same things as generations before. I hated myself. I did not want to live, and I was afraid, so working on our marriage was not possible.

Dusty and I each carried individual wounds needing to be healed, and focusing on the symptoms of a troubled marriage was an ineffective and dangerous distraction. The more we directed our attention toward each other and our relationship, the more vicious the personal attacks became. It was not long before Dusty and I were convinced we had made it through the worst part of the storm, but our pain was deep, and it was difficult to reach. The damage in us was severe, resulting from hideous assaults on our souls (which is why we buried it in the first place). Once all the protective layers were lifted and darkness was exposed from deep within, life became hard for us—and it was not because of our marriage.

Regardless of how we arrived where we were, how hopeless our lives looked on the outside, how scared Dusty and I were on the inside, and how we unintentionally caused others to feel uncomfortable in the midst of our fight for authentic freedom—God was bigger and more powerful. And He is always purposeful. The value and cost of our freedom to trust in Jesus was significant. All we had witnessed and known told us to abandon each other, to move on, and to start over, but we refused. We held on to each other through faith in what we could not see, and our victory was guaranteed as long as we did not let go of Jesus. When we did not have the strength to hold on, it was okay. Our loving Father was holding us anyway, and He was never letting go.

Still, it was ugly. We were good at triggering each other's pain while protecting our own. Dusty would verbally confirm and reinforce the hateful feelings I already felt about myself. I would retaliate with the same, while additionally striking at her fears of abandonment by being silent, not coming home, and remaining detached in a self-medicated state. Pastor Ken eventually admitted he could not help me and recommended a Christian counselor who might. I am grateful for Pastor Ken, and I appreciate what he has done for us. I was unable to see the magnitude of his impact in the midst of our chaos, but he was a significant part in our walk with the Lord. I did not take his admission as giving up on me.

I continued drinking, but I abstained while Dusty and I attended counseling together with a new therapist—James. Our counselor immediately determined we needed to work on individual issues before we approached the problems in our marriage. The plan was for me to stay working with James while Dusty worked on her individual recovery with Jane, a female counselor located within the same office. My wife and I really liked both counselors. Regardless of their diplomas, certifications, designations, and ability to heal their clients, Dusty and I knew they genuinely cared. We appreciated their position of guidance and acknowledgment that if any healing was going to happen, it would be God performing the miracle.

Through the counseling, we made progress, but I also regularly fed my old self through my lawsuit, my drinking, and the lies to keep it all going. Eventually, after a year of cutting back on the amount of alcohol I drank and venturing deeper into my past, I recoiled from pain and fear. Again I went after the mind-numbing booze with abandon, doing my best to expedite the inevitable failure of whatever it was I was trying to do. Even during this, Dusty maintained her focus and continued her painful work, seeking to recover and heal from her past trauma. She remained steadfast in her unwavering determination, and to the best of her ability, she held on to a mustard seed of faith.

Looking back, I am incredibly proud of Dusty and amazed by her courage. It is one thing to embark on a journey into the unknown in an attempt to heal and become whole when you only have yourself to worry about, but Dusty stayed the course while sheltering our children through the consistency of her loving presence. Dusty refused to accept the lie that her window of opportunity to heal had passed. She understood the risk in not doing so was far greater, and she was determined to break the cycle of passing down the compounding generational pain to our children.

Then one day when Dusty and I were scheduled for one of our joint counseling sessions, I did not show up. When I was a lost boy, I looked to the television for places I wanted to live and people I wanted to be like. Now as an adult, I found myself still doing it. A few months prior, I had watched the movie *Leaving Las Vegas* and decided I wanted to end my pain and suffering like the main character in the movie. The story centered on a man who could not quit drinking, who lost his job, and eventually abandoned the family he loved. The man took his severance check, calculating it would be enough to drink himself to death, and went to a place where it would be acceptable to live out the process of dying from alcohol. Like the man in the movie, I wanted to die on the Vegas Strip. I didn't want to live on Sesame Street any longer.

Instead of going to our counseling appointment, I bought my plane ticket to Sin City and checked into a hotel next to the airport, where I would catch my flight early the next morning. I sat alone in the room drinking, wondering if I would even make it on the plane. I took a belt out of my suitcase and cinched it around my neck. I wanted to get a feel for what it would be like if I hung myself in the bathroom. I remember thinking I would have preferred to use the belt my grandfather used to beat my dad and me with, but I accepted the belt I packed as an adequate symbol of our family crest.

While I contemplated suicide in the silence of a hotel room, Dusty became alarmed when I did not show up for our counseling appointment and began to search for me. I am not sure how she did it, but she traced my steps and found me. When she showed up outside my hotel room and began knocking, I sat on the end of my bed and remained quiet, hoping whoever was knocking would go away. But Dusty did not leave, and she kept knocking. When I finally opened the door, I was surprised to see her, yet I felt a peaceful presence when she came in the room. She sat down on the bed next to me and held me while I cried.

Initially, Dusty wasn't sure if she would arrive in time, so she had called the police in advance. The officers showed up at my room shortly after she did, and they questioned me, determining I was no longer a threat to myself or anyone else. I could see the judgment in the officer's eyes, not only toward me but also toward Dusty for remaining by my side. I imagine we were one of the many frustrating domestic calls these men would receive during their shift.

Dusty did not say anything. She held me all night, leaving the decision—whether or not I was going to get on the plane in the morning—to me. By this time, she had gained insight about her issues of codependency, and she knew she could not make me love myself, love her, love our kids, or make good decisions. Those were the very things she had tried to make her parents do when she was a child. I chose not to get on the plane.

I was scared that night, but it had not changed anything. I attended a few more counseling appointments and felt worse. So I bought another ticket to Las Vegas; this time I was going. I picked a day when my schedule was clear of counseling appointments or meetings, a perfect opportunity when Dusty wouldn't expect me home until after the bars had closed. This time, I booked my flight when I could drive directly to the airport and board the plane.

I drank in the airport, I drank on the plane, and I drank for two days straight in Las Vegas. Dusty had no I idea where I was or if I was alive or dead. On the third day, I felt alone and scared, and without thought, I packed my bags, walked out the main lobby, jumped in a cab, and asked the driver to take me to the nearest Urgent Care center. I knew the withdrawals were going to be painful. Much worse was the thought of what I was doing to my wife and three kids. I wished I could give an explanation to those who judged my condition and questioned my behavior. I wished I had an honest answer that made sense. Instead, when asked why, I had no words. Or maybe I knew there was not enough time to tell the whole story. The doctor who treated me called my counselor to let him know I was safe, and my counselor, in turn, let Dusty know I was alive and would be returning home.

CHAPTER 31

—◀◯▶—

All for Nothing

IN SEPTEMBER 2006, I settled my case against Father Chesterfield and the church. In the four years since I had broken my silence and filed the lawsuit, I had attempted to enact my will, to force how I believed the process should unfold, which of course included me receiving what I deserved. It didn't happen that way at all. My plan was not God's best for me.

From the beginning, my Father did not command me to remain silent or to forget my past, especially the little boy I once was. His plan did not include me reliving past childhood abuse while vulnerable and unprotected. My Father did not want me to experience new abuse as a man, in the form of alcohol and drugs. His plan did not involve the continuation of emotional abuse by the one closest to me—someone who constantly spoke lies over me; someone who demanded I hide the guilt and shame; someone who drove me to dark places and inflicted unimaginable pain; someone who was wounded and not yet healed; someone with a broken perspective; someone who believed I deserved the affliction and life sentence. I did not realize it until later, but this someone was me.

If I had fully surrendered to God from the beginning of my journey, I do not know what the process would have looked like. What I do know, and all I need to know, is the abuse would have ended in the exact moment I handed it over to Jesus. I was not required to carry the burden and pay the debt for which Jesus already suffered. My Father would have protected me while I exposed darkness through the light of His son, Jesus Christ. I would not have turned to alcohol to block the memories or drugs to kill the pain when I was weak. Yet my Father so loved me, even though I refused to surrender it all to Him and rejected the payment Jesus already made, He still took my mess and made it good.

When I, along with the many other men involved in the case, arrived at the federal courthouse, staff divided us into groups. One by one, grown men walked into a room behind closed doors to meet with two judges assigned to settle the class action lawsuits. Uncertainty and distrust filled the room that kept us corralled like livestock. Already branded, we now had case numbers to identify each one of us. The court's, church's, and attorney's goal for the day was to settle each claim, forget about the past, issue a check, and then move on.

While I sat in the courtroom, witnessing the vulnerability, brokenness, and transparency of those waiting—each one of us knowing why the others were present—I thought it represented well how Jesus sees the church. We gathered, seeking truth and looking for answers to the desperate question of why we were all lost in a world appearing so big, so apathetic, so answerless. Every one of us was looking for something of genuine value, although many of us were unsure what it was. I was a part of conversations where men described how they received a pass from jail to attend the meeting, and it seemed like they felt more guilt and shame over the childhood abuse than the offenses they had committed as adults. One man was already convicted of murder, and many others were doing time or facing charges for crimes involving drugs and alcohol.

Others attempted to separate themselves by dressing professionally and appearing inconvenienced—I assume to hide the same feelings the rest of us were having. Others in attendance were parents representing a new generation of abused children, too young to attend and defend themselves, along with a few families representing forgotten children who grew up and, unable to move on, chose to end the affliction with suicide. I'm sure many, like me, worried about who we were going to be or where we were going to go once it was over.

Before arriving at the courthouse, I decided to make one final attempt to meet face-to-face with Father Chesterfield. After waiting in the courtroom for hours, my name and number surfaced from the heap of others, and I entered a private room with my attorney, Mr. Lewis, to meet one of the judges. I began by explaining to the Honorable Michael R. Hogan how I had tried everything within my power to put this behind me and move on but was unsuccessful in every attempt. A culmination of events—of dark times and suicidal thoughts—led me to this moment in my life. I argued for the opportunity to confront Father Chesterfield on the basis it was my final option to find closure. As I ended, with Mr. Lewis sitting next to me, I added that in exchange, the church would not have to pay me money but would only be responsible to pay Mr. Lewis' fees.

I could tell Judge Hogan was pressed for time. He made sure not to get sucked into the emotion of my plea, feeling the mounting pressure of the others waiting outside the door for their opportunity to make a request. I continued talking anyway, describing how I wanted Father Chesterfield's time and attention so he could hear from me how hard life had been as a child and how difficult life is now. Judge Hogan responded by asking Mr. Lewis to formalize my offer by putting it in writing and having me sign it.

Judge Hogan then carried my offer to another room, behind closed doors, where representatives of the church, the church's insurance companies, and its lawyers kept a running total of potential monetary damages. When Judge Hogan returned, he said, "I understand you have been asking for this opportunity to meet with Father Chesterfield, but his health is poor, and it is not going to be agreed to by Father Chesterfield, the church, the attorneys, or even the courts."

He encouraged me to discover another way to find closure for myself and then told me the church was willing to offer two hundred thousand dollars to settle the case. Judge Hogan strongly recommended I accept, warning me that a trial was not worth the risk or the ongoing disruption to my life. Judge Hogan did add one more thing, which would remain intentionally omitted from the settlement documents. He told me if I were to accept the offer, he would do something for me—something precluded without a formal confession or conviction by the accused. He explained that if I was willing to write a letter to Father Chesterfield, communicating in written form the words I would tell him in person, he would read it to Father Chesterfield personally.

I was alone with Mr. Lewis to deliberate my decision. He advised me to accept the offer and settle. I spent the evening talking it over with Dusty, reflecting on the previous years and the way in which, through the process, I had lost control of my life. I felt like a failure, and I could not recognize the blessing of my wife and children, who remained with me through it all. I could not see Jesus extending His hand, willing to take the entire burden from me. I simply resigned myself to what I perceived as defeat. Father Chesterfield and the church had won again. All the work, sacrifice, and tears I had poured into proving I was something, the fight to be validated, and the vulnerable telling of the truth—it had all been for nothing. Instead, they backed me into a corner with only one option—to give up.

"I accept the offer, Judge Hogan," I told the judge in person and then began to cry. To my surprise, Judge Hogan hugged me and held his embrace for what seemed like an hour. *This is more meaningful than anything I have experienced during the entire process,* I thought to myself. In settling, I accepted the money and the judge's offer to read a letter I would write to Father Chesterfield.

I wrote the letter, and Mr. Lewis provided it to Judge Hogan. After a few months, I made calls to Mr. Lewis seeking confirmation that Father Chesterfield had heard my words spoken by someone else. Many more months passed with no word. Finally, I wrote a letter to the judge and provided a document for him to sign confirming that he in fact had read the letter. On December 19, 2007, I received the following letter from Judge Hogan:

> *Dear Mr. Rossman:*
>
> *This will acknowledge receipt of your recent letter. I read your letter to Father Chesterfield many months ago at his retirement residence. I believe the date was Friday, November 3, 2006.*
>
> *Sincerely,*
> *Michael R. Hogan*
> *United States District Judge*

After deducting reimbursable attorney costs and Mr. Lewis' percentage of the settlement proceeds, I did not have enough to pay my debts or secure my family's future. But I did have more than enough to fund my ongoing pursuit of death.

CHAPTER 32

—◁◦▷—

The Beginning of the End

ALCOHOL COULD NO LONGER numb the pain. It was not enough. I was a regular at a biker bar, even though I did not own a motorcycle or look the part. What I did have was tolerance for large quantities of booze and enough money to pay for my own drinks, as well as rounds for everyone else. During one of my binges, I sat next to a man who offered me a pill. I didn't know what it was or what it would do. He offered it to me no differently than one would offer someone a breath mint. Without hesitation, I took it as if it were candy. However, unlike candy, this pill took away my pain immediately. It was the beginning of the end for me, and I began to mix the deadly combination of painkillers and whiskey over the next six months.

Each day, I would return home after the bars closed, full of booze and pills, and crawl into bed next to my wife and pass out. Understandably fed up with my behavior, Dusty was near the end of her rope. But worse, she was heartbroken and scared, left alone to raise our two kids. During this time, I also stopped spending time with my son, Cole, who more than likely interpreted it as rejection because of something he had done.

One night, after I stumbled into our bedroom and lay down next to Dusty in silence, she noticed the intervals of my breathing change. The periods of me not breathing began to increase, and Dusty called

911. Before she did, she paused, not because she wanted me to die, but because she knew I did want to die. She knew how angry I would be with her when I discovered she had intervened in my opportunity to die without suffering.

My family and I were now living in our newest building, and our two-story loft was on the top floor. The building had twenty-four units that were occupied by people I had come to know. All the units were accessible through the main lobby, elevator, and common corridors. The fire truck and ambulance arrived, with sirens blaring and lights flashing, waking up the community around three in the morning. Through the corridor, down the elevator, and out the main lobby, while debilitated by an overdose, I was lifted into the ambulance and driven to the emergency room.

Dusty arranged for someone to watch our kids and then joined me at the hospital. When she arrived, the attending physician told her I would have died if she hadn't made the call. He also asked if she knew what pills I was taking, telling her I would not share the information with him or the nurse. Dusty, however, didn't know; she wasn't even aware I had been taking pills.

After a brief stay in the emergency room, the attending physician released me to go home. A few hours later, I woke up at my regular time, in my own bed, and began my normal morning routine. As I stood at the edge of our bed, I saw Dusty staring at me with a confused look. At the same time, I noticed a hospital band around my wrist. Equally confused, I asked her if I had gone to the hospital. I possessed no recollection of her 911 call, the firefighters, the paramedics, or the hospital. Dusty explained what had transpired only a few hours before. In response, I said nothing. I took a shower, got dressed, and went to work for a few hours. Then I went right back to drinking and taking pills.

I still was not going to church, and I stopped going to counseling. I gave up hope. Even my counselor, James, made the familiar admission—he would not be able to help me. My friend, John, also acknowledged he did not know how to help me, and I stopped meeting with him. Dusty's counselor, Jane, challenged her to draw a line for her own well-being, to say she had had enough. Dusty was desperate. She understood it was only a matter of time before I killed someone while driving under the influence or died of an overdose. Out of options, but unwilling to give up on me, she began to research setting up an intervention, along with sending me to a treatment center with a faith-based program focused on trauma recovery. Dusty forcefully pled with the person in admissions for an immediate intervention, but even those plans would need to be stepped up.

Wanting to see my kids, I came home uncharacteristically early one afternoon. Because I would often leave the house before my wife and kids got up in the morning and would not return home until they were asleep in bed, I had not seen them for some time. When I walked into our loft and sat on the couch, my kids ran to me, full of love and excitement to see their dad. Sophia and Luke jumped into my arms and onto my lap. Dusty, who was surprised to see me, sat down next to the three of us quietly, purposefully allowing the moment to happen without dragging our pain into their joy. Then, quietly, with my head tipped back and my family all around me, I stopped breathing. Dusty called 911.

The same firefighters and paramedics responded and quickly got me breathing again. While they were loading me onto the gurney, one of the men asked Dusty how much more she was going to take. How much more of my reckless behavior was she willing to expose our children to? This time, Dusty did not rush to the hospital. She waited for someone to call her to come pick me up. When she arrived, the doctor and nurse looked at her as if she were a fool and at me as if I were trash.

My wife set the intervention date for January 12, 2009. She met with the intervention specialist, who flew out on short notice from the East Coast, along with my mom, dad, Pastor Ken, James, Jane, John, and my business partner. To ensure I would be home, Dusty asked if I would stay with the kids the following morning while she went to her counseling appointment. No counseling appointment was scheduled. Instead, my intervention was going to take place. Unaware of her plan, I agreed.

It was early morning; I sat at our dining room table, feeling the onset of withdrawal while making a to-do list. I itemized the impossible tasks I needed to accomplish in order to keep my life from completely falling apart. At the time, Dusty and I were in the final phases of completing construction on our new dream house. I was also in the middle of building retail space for three new businesses, one of which was Dusty's new salon that she would be opening and operating. And I was in the final steps of working out the terms on a loan with a bank for the development company. It was a hopeless exercise. I knew I could not stay sober or alive long enough to complete any of my responsibilities. While I held my head in my hands, the front door opened, and everyone entered. Immediately I knew what was happening, and relief washed over me.

Without a thought, I surrendered in my heart to the intervention process and the anticipated invitation to receive help. But before help was offered, I listened to heartfelt yet forthright letters by those participating. I was all ears as one by one they shared how much they cared about me and how my addiction, poor choices, and behavior adversely affected them. What I heard was true, and I listened intently. My mom described how much I hurt her when I told her I wished she was dead. My dad cried, explaining he would no longer tolerate a drunk because of what his alcoholic father did to him. My business partner described how my addiction and alcohol abuse put his family's financial security at risk. Pastor Ken, James, Jane, and a few of my friends expressed their concern, saying they wanted me to get help. Finally, John, in typical nonconforming fashion, did not follow the instructions. He calmly read Scripture. I do not remember what book, chapter, or verse it was, but I remember knowing the words were not a judgment or a manipulative condemnation. They were truth, and my Father's loving words moved me more than all others.

Within hours, I was on a plane to Laguna Beach, California, to enter my fifth treatment center. Like before, as soon as the doors closed behind me, I no longer needed a drink. I felt safe. The program was not any different from the others, and my thirty days went by too quickly. I was not ready to walk out the doors, not even for a stroll on the beach, and reenter a world already proven an adversary I could not conquer on my own. However, there was one thing different about this place, and it wasn't the beautiful ocean across the street, a guaranteed program for sobriety, or a secret to success in life. Rather, it was a young woman.

The previous facilities where I had sought help had not admitted anyone like her. I noticed her during a recovery-based Bible study, where she started acting out. As a young woman in her early twenties, Abigail carried the burden of a painful past. She suffered deeply from her wounds and could care less what others thought of her or her actions. Her pain and suffering outweighed the judgment. While others laughed, became scared, or felt uncomfortable, her cry for help actually made sense to me.

Unable to hide his own discomfort, the counselor leading the small group asked Abigail what was going on. Without hesitation, she explained the constant attacks by spirits throwing fiery darts at her. It was clear, Abigail hadn't experienced a life that was protected; no one shielded her from attacks; no one listened. Because of her experiences, which left her in perpetual vulnerability and exposure, she had nowhere to hide. She began to cry—not because of the threats of what would happen if she told her secret, but because of the hopelessness of knowing her plea for help would go unheard.

When she was a child, Abigail's innocence and purity hadn't lasted long enough for her to understand their value—her value. The void in her soul darkened, causing her to believe that there was nowhere to run and no one to run to. She experienced unending trauma in a fallen world, and she held secrets to stories she did not ask to be a part of. Other than the cut marks on her wrists, Abigail did not have visible scars to show others how bad it was for her. The symptoms of pain made her unbelievable. She learned to survive without basic credibility as a hurting child of God. Abigail could no longer conform to the world's scale that measured value based only on what was visible. It was all she had ever known, and based on her broken perspective, she made choices. She was unprotected and vulnerable.

In observing Abigail, I could see she was unable to trust. She didn't trust the staff, she didn't trust a few other women in the program who showed her genuine kindness, and she didn't trust the process. Rather, Abigail drifted to others in the program, who in turn descended on her. From her perspective, she knew what a select few wanted from her, and in her mind, she could control what was going to happen to her. It wasn't long before Abigail was out of the program for sexual contact with a few of the male patients, who hid their own secrets, knew what to look for, and knew how to take advantage of her damaged soul.

As the thirty days came to a close, I stalled and hoped for a miracle in my life. I needed more time; walking out the doors meant I would die. There was the miracle I wanted from my Father—the one where I would need to fully surrender my life and my will over to His care. Yet while I still contemplated whether I was even capable of letting go, I sensed I was still willing to settle for the elusive answer the majority of people claimed to possess, but I was unable to grasp. Starting over and trying harder remained an option. I moved to a less intensive facility in Palm Springs, but it was still an institution closed off to life, where I didn't need to drink or take pills to cope with my fears. The thirty days there went by too quickly once again, and I stayed for another round.

Finally, out of insurance benefits and out of options but unwilling and unable to return to my old life, I returned to Laguna Beach and moved into a sober living house. The halfway house did not possess the same institutionalized security the recovery centers seemed to provide, and I felt like the frightened five-year-old boy I was when I moved to a new neighborhood. I felt my vulnerability made me a target, and I was stricken with shame at who I was—a scared man. I only lasted one night. The next day, I moved out, checked into a hotel, and got drunk.

I sent Dusty and John an email letting them know what had happened and where I was. John responded with a late night call and asked if I would be willing to get on a plane the next morning and fly home. He offered to pick me up from the airport and take me to a place where he, along with a group of men, would pray for me. I was drunk when we spoke, but I remember the conversation clearly. Much of what came out of my mouth while intoxicated was an attempt to hide pain and conceal the truth about who I believed I was. My drunken outbursts, fed by anger and the resentments I was unable to shake, provided a temporary release.

Yet at times, the underlying truth emerged through my slurred manifestos, which is exactly what happened during our conversation. I said something to John that held the secret to my continued suffering. It was the critical belief holding me back and undermining the valid work I had done and the life-giving gifts within reach. It was what was keeping me in the cycle of fear, my own bad choices, and the grip of the Enemy. What I told John was, "I knew you would be the one to help me some day."

My friend, John, did help me on my journey. Most importantly, he introduced me to Jesus. However, just as I fantasized about a savior as a hurting and frightened child, as an adult, I continued to look for my savior in a man. I unfairly placed the impossible burden on John and expected him to fix things within me and around me. I loved him, admired his unwavering belief in God, and wanted the same freedom he experienced. However, I could not have it until I let go of my childhood fantasy. Only then could I discover for myself the only way to freedom and the Father.

The only way to freedom was not through John, my dad, performance, or alcohol and painkillers; it was only through Jesus. Until I accepted truth, I wasn't going to change. I would not be free. I needed to experience and trust in the truth that my Father was always listening to me, He knew my pain and my joy, and I could always run to Him. He loved me where I was at all times and in every condition. I couldn't rely on someone else to do this for me. My relationship with Jesus had to be direct, unique, and only mine. Counsel from trusted men is good, but I needed to receive the truth from Jesus because my life depended on it. Only He could truly save me.

Although Jesus was leading me in to freedom from the bondage of my past, I wasn't ready to see from faith yet.

John picked me up from the airport, and as we had agreed, I did not drink. We drove to his office, where five men waited to pray for me. Some of the men I already knew, and others I met for the first time. I was comfortable and felt I was among brothers.

They spoke words of encouragement over me, gave me a father's blessing, broke off the lies, prayed to restore authority to its rightful place, declared hope over me, and read Scripture, highlighting God's power and intention to guide and strengthen me in His love. I crawled into the room with those men on that day, and there Jesus lifted me up. To the best of my ability, I took my next step by forgiving each person who sinned against me and asking that I might be forgiven by those whom I had sinned against. Through the process, I entered deeper into the kingdom of heaven and closer to receiving my promised freedom.

I wish my story consisted only of the previous paragraph. I wish my testimony was an account of a brief and challenging season followed by a miracle delivering me from the storm. For some, it happens more quickly. However, I know God has a plan and purpose for each person's testimony. He is more than capable of using my painful journey to help others along their journeys. If I did not believe God's Word, I would not have written this book. I spent too many years forgetting my past and wishing my life away. Now I know when I find Jesus in it, He can use my story to bring freedom to others.

When I returned home, Dusty greeted me at the door and gave me a big hug. She looked into my eyes and said I looked different. She noticed a clarity and vividness to the blue where before there was only gray. I had gained wisdom to know I was different and eyes to see my life and our family restored. Over the next months and years, each of us, individually with Jesus, battled our demons and allowed Him to heal our wounds. Together, with Jesus by our sides, we remained committed to our marriage. Through His healing in our lives, we built a new foundation to stand our lives upon. At last, we were fully equipped to move on and begin a new journey, building a new inheritance with a lasting legacy for our children.

CHAPTER 33

—◀◉▶—

Free at Last

ONE MORNING, AS I sat in my office, I felt prompted to open the newspaper to the obituaries. I no longer scanned the death notices on a daily basis. Months had passed since the last time I read about various crimes, and I had gained a different perspective on all the people involved, understanding it would no longer help me feel better about myself. Calmly, I thumbed through the pages, feeling covered by peace, until I arrived at the obituaries. My eyes went directly to Father Chesterfield's brief obituary. There was no mention of his lifelong commitment to God, his good works, or any family members left behind. The obituary held no reflection on fond memories, but only his name, birth date, and the date of his death, along with the details of a small memorial service. I folded the paper and thanked God I had nothing to do with his death.

In the months leading up to my increased awareness of God's plan for each of us, Dusty and I had received a new perspective on who we were in the eyes of Jesus, and through our process, we experienced the gift of knowing who our Father had always been, who He was today, and who He would be tomorrow. Life is different with a Father who loves perfectly, who listens even when there are no words spoken, who affirms when the world rejects, and who is forever present. He never grows weary of our stumbling efforts to discover His will and His perfect plan for our lives. The walk with

Jesus allows us time, in the glory of authentic freedom, to breathe and rest in the assurance of His love and the wisdom to know God is in control.

Dusty and I were moving on to a season of letting go and unwinding areas in our lives that bound us to a life we were going to leave behind—but not forget. We decided to begin taking our steps with increased faith and, to the best of our abilities, obedience to our Father's loving guidance. We committed to growing in our capacity to confront the giants in our lives and not retreat when faced with fear and the threat of pain.

Personally, I began the process by separating from my business partner and dividing the remaining properties for which we shared ownership. My dad had already retired after the last project, and we were no longer working together. I knew God was not instructing me to abandon my obligations and responsibilities, but I sensed these business connections I had established as my old self did not align with God's purposes for the next season of my life.

The debt obligations for me and Dusty were over fifteen million dollars, and at the peak of the real estate market, it was well secured on paper. After the housing market crashed and the financial markets followed, the effects of over-leveraging doomed Sesame Street. I spent the next two years working with lenders to minimize the losses that would follow. I maintained and managed the buildings through the grueling process, while at the same time draining all of our personal assets. It was an intentional exercise of full disclosure, with no attempt to hide what I had to contribute. After short sales and an uncontested foreclosure, the remaining obligation was down to $370,000. With the bank at the end of its lawful ability to forgive, along with its fiduciary responsibility to shareholders, Dusty and I were required to make payments we could not make, and in 2012, we filed for bankruptcy.

Dusty didn't blame me for our financial situation. She didn't tell me, "If only you had done this ..." or "If only you had not done that ...." Instead, Dusty provided me with unwavering support, words of encouragement, and loving reminders that our Father was in complete control. Her unconditional love and commitment to stand with me through a difficult time was not her first display of courage, character, and loyalty, but it was the first time that I opened my heart and received it. I arrived through the fire, and on the other side of darkness—as a thankful and humble man—I began to experience the gifts of being married to my partner, friend, and loving wife. As the imprisonment of a false protection crumbled, despite my occasional fearful retreats, and as I learned to let go of old beliefs through increased faith and trust in Jesus, I always received much more. Relative to my growing capacity to steward the gifts I longed for, peace and freedom were always in reach. I grabbed on to them each time with a deep understanding of their cost and eternal value.

In the midst of all this, Dusty and I were attending Sunday services once again, along with a weekly home group. The small gathering was a more intimate setting, where we spent time worshipping, sharing testimonies, and listening to an online video stream from a church in California. The weekly messages resonated with me, as the pastors who preached spoke truth of Jesus, the Father, and His love for me. Truth was spoken, and Jesus gloriously appeared, aligning with the love, mercy, grace, and forgiveness that I experienced through my journey. I realized in a whole new measure the truth of His goodness, and I claimed His promises. It reinforced my growing dependence, relationship, and trust in Him.

I found hope in knowing the world really was as I experienced it—not in a way specific to the abuse, but in the sense that it wasn't intended to replace my heavenly Father. I was not going to change fact by collaborating in lawsuits, force, deception, and bargaining. Trials and tribulations were not going away through the deception of a magic bottle or pill, and victory and freedom would remain unattainable through reliance on my performance, financial success, or the high esteem of others. However, I also discovered that by believing in my savior, by growing in faith, by engaging in prayer, and by choosing to live my life in God's foundational truth in order to glorify Him—I really could experience heaven on earth.

Not long after we began listening to the messages from this church in California, in the fall of 2009, Dusty and I attended a conference in Redding, California, home to the church we were watching online. Aside from the sunshine we both loved, the beautiful backdrop of majestic mountains and the Sacramento River, Dusty and I discovered something special during the weeklong event. We found an incredibly honoring environment within an atmosphere of hope. After our journey over the previous eight years, we were nothing less than two sponges exposed to the truth of God's kingdom.

Dusty and I talked about how we would love our children to be in a school environment where the value of all kids was measured through the eyes of Jesus—seeing them as the priceless treasures they were. Before any other lesson was taught, students first learned how much Jesus loved them, and because of a sovereign truth, they had the ability to discern the lies the world attempted to press upon them. Early on, children were intentionally equipped with the power to rebuke anything that did not align with the Father's loving words, which covered them daily. Thus, they knew they were something and would always be something. Their promised freedom was secure under the protection of a loving God. They were free to dream big. The belief that all things are possible through Jesus became their normal.

As we considered these things, Dusty and I discussed someday moving to Redding, dreaming about having our kids attend the Christian school there. We knew it would not be the sole responsibility of the church and its staff to teach our children. We needed to live out these same truths on a daily basis in our home in order to continue building an inheritance for our children and future generations. For the first time in our lives, in order to fulfill our dreams, we did not need to start over. Starting over meant going back to the beginning, but we had already done that. Painstakingly, we had gone through the slow and methodical process of replacing each lie from our pasts with the truth, and we had come out the other side knowing our Father had never forsaken us. Our solid foundation was now set on the life of Jesus. What we were now free to talk about was exercising faith, embracing the true gift of freedom, reclaiming through Jesus what was once lost, and receiving our rightful inheritance.

"Someday," we said, dreaming aloud, "maybe when we have all our ducks in a row and the time is right, then we can make such a bold move." Okay, maybe we were not quite exercising faith yet, but we were definitely stretching the idea.

When Dusty and I returned from California, I continued navigating the entanglement of a relatively complex business and identity that had turned upside down. I felt conflicted at times, wanting to save the business and reestablish my identity, yet also desiring to honor my obligations and ultimately to be free. I knew I needed to be careful about how I defined the freedom I was pursuing. It could not be freedom from my circumstances or the fear of failure. Rather, I needed freedom to breathe, to do the things I was capable of doing in order to meet my obligations and begin living the life God intended me to live. My walk with Jesus could not be dependent upon whether the business succeeded or failed. Thus, I asked and trusted the things in my life that were encumbering God's plan would be purged, or that He would reveal it was time for me to let them go. It was an exercise of patience. I stood in the fire sober, while I was formed to steward greater and more abundant gifts, the greatest of which were treasures I already possessed.

The process was not easy, and I was not perfect. But the path I took was different, and I was my old imperfect self less often. I was learning to live freely in a less than perfect body with a less than perfect mind in a less than perfect world. My problem was not that I believed I was perfect, but rather I was convinced I needed to be. When I slipped, Jesus, who is perfect, was quick to hold me up and keep me from falling into the cycle of self-condemnation. I remembered my past, a time when I tried to prove I was who others said I was—not who my Father made me to be. Now, with my self-will and fear cast out, I deeply desired not to return to my old life. My new and preferred choice was to do those things honoring God.

In the summer of 2010, Dusty, Sophia, Luke, and I all made a trip to Redding for a few days to enjoy the hot sun and to give the kids a chance to swim as much as their hearts desired. It was a last minute trip, and while we were there, without any definitive plans or expectations, Dusty placed Sophia and Luke on the Christian school's waiting list for the fall. She believed it was a safe and harmless exercise of her freedom to dream—not only for herself but also for our children and our family. There was nothing to worry about, she explained, adding that the list was long, and Sophia and Luke were somewhere near the bottom.

After our return home, we quickly settled into our current normalcy, which by most standards was becoming increasingly less normal. One day, during bedtime prayer, unprovoked by any mention of the subject, Sophia prayed the following five-year-old prayer, "I pray for a spot to open in the Redding school today, tomorrow, or the next day."

Dusty thought it was a precious and cute prayer by our sweet girl and then proceeded to discount the childlike faith quietly in her mind. But on the second day after Sophia's prayer, my wife received a phone call from the school's staff.

"Is this Dusty Rossman?" the woman asked.

After Dusty answered in the affirmative, the woman identified herself as calling from Bethel Christian School and said, "We have a spot open for both Sophia and Luke if you would like to reserve them." If we did want the openings, she told Dusty, we needed to have Sophia attend an introductory meeting with her new teacher in two days.

Later that day, Dusty casually told me, "I received a call today from the school in California. There are spots open for both kids. What should we do?"

We both knew what we wanted to do, and we knew what we would have done in the past. This time we chose differently. We saw God had opened a door, and we were going to walk through it, even though we had no idea what was on the other side. School started in two weeks. "What should we do?" We were moving to Redding, California. It so happened to be where we had stopped to get our marriage license seven years before. *This has to be a sign, or at least a wonder,* I thought. I did wonder how it was all going to work.

At the time, there was still a remote possibility that the properties we owned could be retained, and I was in constant meetings with lenders. Dusty and I also owned a salon where she operated the business and serviced her long-term clients. We did not have a backup plan for the eventual loss of all our businesses and our source of income, and the economy was in the middle of the worst recession since the Great Depression. We had depleted all our assets and had no money apart from the small salary I was paying myself to manage the properties. The money Dusty earned in the salon went to pay rent on the retail space, which went to the bank, which went toward the payment on the mortgage we placed on the building.

The logical thing would have been to delay the move until we had all our personal and business affairs under control—or to not move at all. We were facing some pressing issues, to say the least. When we held those issues up against a dream, something Dusty and I had little practice in doing, it appeared impossible. Yet as much as our desire to move didn't make sense, there was another reality confronting me, making the others seem insignificant. Our step into faith would lead me to face the most difficult decision of my life. Moving to Redding would mean moving away from my son Cole. It was a dilemma I didn't want to face. I didn't want to live at a distance from my beloved son, yet I could not ignore the open door and the possibility awaiting us if we followed God's invitation. It was a hard decision to make, but we decided to go. Even now, I do not understand it all, but I trust God to work it out for our good.

Dusty and the kids moved first, getting a jump on the few remaining days before Sophia and Luke started school. Dusty also needed to find us a place to live. I followed them soon after. I needed to make monthly trips north to check on the properties, but for the most part, I spent every day with Dusty, Sophia, and Luke. The income from the properties barely covered our living expenses, but for the first time, I had a lot of time with my family. I quickly discovered I loved being around my wife and kids, and they loved being around me. Over the next year and a half, God began restoring the time we had lost as a family. He restored the days and nights I had wasted away from home.

I began to look deeply within myself and, for the first time, I began to love more than I despised. I looked at Dusty, Sophia, and Luke—and thought of Cole—feeling the authentic love I had always felt for them but had not been able to express. Because I had finally learned to love myself, I was free to love them, too. I missed Cole dearly and still do. But instead of blocking out the pain, I choose to embrace my unwavering hope that God will restore my time with him as well.

Cole is and always has been a precious gift, and I treasure him in my heart and daily thoughts. I am proud to be his dad. He is infinitely valuable simply because of who he is and because he is my son. But I have a special thankfulness for him in my heart because, if it had not been for him, I may not have remembered the lost boy I once was. Cole's innocence would not allow me to forget and move on without him. Because of him and my Father in heaven, I finally found the peace and freedom my heart always longed for.

Made in the USA
San Bernardino, CA
20 September 2016